ETpedia™
Management

500 ideas for managing an English Language school

guidance

decisions

planning

professional development

Fiona Dunlop, Keith Harding and Robert McLarty

Series editor: John Hughes

www.myetpedia.com

ETpedia Management
500 ideas for managing an English language school

© Pavilion Publishing & Media

The authors have asserted their rights in accordance with the Copyright, Designs and Patents Act (1988) to be identified as the authors of this work.

Published by:
Pavilion Publishing and Media Ltd
Blue Sky Offices
Cecil Pashley Way
Shoreham by Sea
West Sussex
BN43 5FF
UK
Tel: 01273 434 943
Fax: 01273 227 308

First published 2019

All rights reserved. No part of this publication may be reproduced, stored in a retrieval system, or transmitted in any form or by any means, electronic, mechanical, photocopying, recording or otherwise, without the prior permission in writing of the publisher and the copyright owners. A catalogue record for this book is available from the British Library.

Photocopying permission

The resources in the Appendix may be copied, without fee or prior permission, by the purchaser subject to both of the following conditions: that the item is reproduced in its entirety, including the copyright acknowledgement; that the copies are used solely by the person or organisation who purchased the original publication.

ISBN: 978-1-912755-27-1
PDF ebook ISBN: 978-1-912755-74-5
Epub ISBN: 978-1-912755-73-8
Kindle ISBN: 978-1-912755-75-2

Authors: Fiona Dunlop, Keith Harding and Robert McLarty
Editor: Penny Hands
Production editor: Mike Benge, Pavilion Publishing and Media
Cover design: Emma Dawe, Pavilion Publishing and Media
Page layout and typesetting: Tony Pitt, Pavilion Publishing and Media
Printing: Ashford Press

Contents

Introduction

- 10 facts about the authors 6
- 10 reasons for using this resource 7
- 10 ways to use this resource 9

Getting started

- Unit 1: 10 things you need to know about management 12
- Unit 2: 10 misconceptions people have about managers 15
- Unit 3: 10 areas of management in ELT 18
- Unit 4: 10 roles and responsibilities in an ideal management team 21
- Unit 5: 10 transferable skills for teachers who want to be managers 24
- Unit 6: 10 external organisations and partners you need to work with 27
- Unit 7: 10 conversations that need to happen in your school 30
- Unit 8: 10 questions to ask about strategic management 33
- Unit 9: 10 ways to ensure an organisation is dynamic 36
- Unit 10: 10 ways to encourage team-building and team morale 39
- Unit 11: 10 reasons why meetings don't work 41
- Unit 12: 10 things you can do with a decision 44
- Unit 13: 10 reasons why change may fail 46
- Unit 14: 10 tips for making HR human 49
- Unit 15: 10 steps to successful recruitment 52
- Unit 16: 10 ways of achieving staff loyalty 55
- Unit 17: 10 tips for writing policy statements and the staff handbook 58
- Unit 18: 10 principles of efficient student administration 61
- Unit 19: 10 things you can expect from technology 64
- Unit 20: 10 ways of promoting your organisation 67
- Unit 21: 10 ways of making an impact on a target market 70
- Unit 22: 10 ways of networking and using social media 73
- Unit 23: 10 ways of developing new products 76

Unit 24: 10 ideas you can borrow from other sectors 79

Unit 25: 10 financial concepts everyone should know 82

Unit 26: 10 checks to ensure cost-effectiveness 85

Unit 27: 10 things you can do when times are bad 88

Unit 28: 10 things your customers expect 91

Unit 29: 10 early stages in the student journey 94

Unit 30: 10 types of feedback 97

Unit 31: 10 things you can do with feedback 100

Unit 32: 10 tips for dealing with complaints 103

Unit 33: 10 ways of turning 'OK' into 'Wow!' 105

Unit 34: 10 points to remember when planning a new course 108

Unit 35: 10 principles behind timetable planning 111

Unit 36: 10 ways of ensuring and measuring student progress 114

Unit 37: 10 ways of improving the quality of teaching 117

Unit 38: 10 ways of doing lesson observations 120

Unit 39: 10 tips for effective appraisals 123

Unit 40: 10 ways of monitoring and rewarding staff performance 126

Unit 41: 10 ways of encouraging professional development for teachers 128

Unit 42: 10 ways to ensure professional development achieves something 131

Unit 43: 10 ideas for managing your own professional development 134

Unit 44: 10 tips for managing yourself 137

Unit 45: 10 ways of networking and developing your own career 140

Unit 46: 10 non-academic services you may need to provide 143

Unit 47: 10 ways to improve your working environment 146

Unit 48: 10 ways to ensure your premises are conducive to learning 149

Unit 49: 10 key points in safeguarding and well-being 152

Unit 50: 10 things you hope to hear when students (and staff) leave 155

Appendix **159**

Introduction

10 facts about the authors

Fiona Dunlop…

- ▶ has taught in Egypt, Brazil and the UK. She has been a director of studies, teacher trainer, academic director and school principal.
- ▶ has delivered teacher and management training in a large number of countries including Chile, Kurdistan, Georgia, Spain and Brazil. She has a particular passion for professional development and believes strongly in her own lifelong learning.
- ▶ is currently the Principal of Wimbledon School of English in London. She has worked there for 18 years.

Keith Harding…

- ▶ has worked as a teacher, teacher trainer, director of studies and school principal in the UK and the US, and has delivered ELT management courses in the Middle East, South America and Europe.
- ▶ has authored or co-authored coursebooks on business English, English for tourism and English for specific purposes.
- ▶ has been an inspector for Accreditation UK (British Council) since 2007. He is a tutor on the Trinity Diploma in ELT Management.

Robert McLarty…

- ▶ has taught in France, New Zealand and the UK. He has been a director of studies at International House, School Principal at OISE, a publishing manager at OUP and a principal academic staff member at Wintec.
- ▶ has co-authored coursebooks, workbooks and methodology titles for OUP, CUP, Pearson and Pavilion ELT.
- ▶ is currently living in New Zealand and is editor of *Modern English Teacher*.

All three authors…

believe in the importance of an approach to management that is both professional and practical and which works to the benefit of all stakeholders, including students, teachers, administrative and other staff, as well as managers themselves.

10 reasons for using this resource

1. **Everything in one place**
   There have been thousands of books written about management but very few written specifically with English language teaching in mind. There are also many blogs, websites, videos and articles offering advice on how to be a manager, but not one resource which brings all the key advice together in one place. That's the aim of *ETpedia Management*. It's a collection of resources for anyone involved in ELT management to consult whenever they need to.

2. **Clearly organised**
   This resource contains 50 units and is divided into eight sections covering the key areas of current ELT management. Each section contains a number of units with each unit offering ten tips. Why ten? Well, we believe that knowing ten skills that are transferable from a teaching role into management will be enough to help you to make the move into management; reading about ten ways of making an impact in a new market will encourage you and your school make such a move if you choose to; and knowing ten things to do when things start to go wrong financially will always be useful, should the need arise.

3. **Preparing for an interview**
   If you are applying for a managerial position, read the sections that are relevant to your potential role. Interviewers for management positions are interested in your experience, but they are also keen to hear ideas for situations you may not have encountered.

4. **Training for a new management position**
   If you're starting a new position, you will be given training and advice on the role. Looking at the ETpedia tips alongside any in-house support will help enrich your understanding of the role and what's involved.

5. **Studying for an ELT management qualification**
   If you're studying for a diploma in ELT Management or taking the subject as a module on a master's programme, you'll find that this resource complements the materials provided or recommended. The lists will be useful for brainstorming with other participants or for using as an aide-memoire when writing assignments.

6. **On your own**
   You may find yourself in quite an isolated management position, responsible for a specific group of teachers in a particular location. This might be at home or abroad, working antisocial hours and possibly with very little support. If this is you, use this resource to brief yourself on any topics you are unsure of – or simply to reinforce what you already felt.

7. **Troubleshooting and firefighting**
   There are times when a problem emerges that you need to deal with quickly. The course of action to take may not come to you instantly. Referring to the appropriate section or unit of this book may provide the answer, or at least get you thinking about practical approaches that will solve the situation.

8. **Building awareness of the manager role**

   In some schools, the manager can be seen as a distant figure living in a separate world from that of the teachers and administrative staff 'on the ground'. To mitigate against this, hold meetings or workshops with the teachers and administrative staff, where you all look at a unit or section of the book and talk about the manager's role. Many of the units include reflective tasks which can be carried out together with your staff.

9. **Ideas for improving and updating existing systems in your school**

   All managers inherit or develop systems to suit a particular era, set of students or cohort of teachers. There comes a time when those systems need to be reviewed and amended. This resource will give you a starting point for such a review. It will provide food for thought and checklists of points to consider.

10. **More ideas from managers around the world**

    Throughout this resource you will find further ideas in the form of quotes from a wide range of managers working in all sorts of schools throughout the world. Their thoughts on a particular topic are all based on recent and real experience as ELT managers.

> *"I know personally that the transition from teaching to management can be highly rewarding as well as challenging. You will have to adjust quickly but if you get the opportunity just go for it. The ETpedia management resource provides an excellent roadmap for making the move both manageable and exciting."*
>
> **Huan Japes, Membership Director, English UK**

10 ways to use this resource

This book is for teachers and managers at different stages of their managerial career. They might be teachers who have aspirations for management, people who have recently been given a managerial role or task, or managers with many years of experience. It also aims to help other people understand the manager role and to encourage them to consider ELT management as a career step. For these reasons, you can use this book in different ways.

1. **Cover to cover**
   Start at the beginning and read it unit by unit to get an overview of the practical aspects of various management sectors and roles. This will show you the diversity and range of the managerial role – and how exciting and interesting the job can be.

2. **Read a specific section**
   You may be responsible for or interested in a particular area. Perhaps you've been tasked with introducing a fresh approach to professional development or improving the way you gather and handle feedback. If so, then focus on that section to develop your ideas, modifying the tips to suit your own context.

3. **Dipping in for ideas**
   There will be times in your working life when you are short of ideas but looking for something to spark a change in your school. If that is the case, open the book at random and read a few tips. You will be bound to find something to interest and inspire you, and your school will see the benefits.

4. **Read it again**
   The first time you read this book might be as a new manager. After you've been doing the job for a while, read it again. You're likely to take something different from it every time you do.

5. **Write in the book**
   Treat the resource a little like a recipe book. Read a unit, take your own notes and try things out. Reflect on your experience by noting things down. Over time your copy of the book will become an even more useful resource and something you can use as you recruit new managers yourself.

6. **Use the Appendix**
   You'll see this icon beside tips that have an accompanying photocopiable document in the Appendix. This might be an activity for you to use as part of your own teacher development in-house, or a template for a document you need to write as a manager, such as an observation form or an HR policy.

7. **Activities and reflective tasks**
   This icon often appears at the end of a unit. It denotes an activity or reflective task that will help you develop your managerial culture and style. Activities can be done individually or collectively. They will not only focus your mind on various aspects of your job, but also help you to build a more holistic culture for your school.

8. Help and advise colleagues

One of the key roles of a manager is to identify talent and develop staff. You may want to use certain units of the resource as specific guidance and support for people you work with, such as your senior teachers or co-ordinators. Refer them to relevant parts of the book as part of their ongoing development, or to help with a particular issue.

9. Experiment with something different

You're unlikely to be able to implement every point in this book, and in any case there will be many that you feel are not relevant. But it's always good to try out something that's a bit different and out of your comfort zone. If it works, you've got a new approach. If it doesn't, you could try another one – or you might conclude that your existing approach was the best all along.

10. Write your own 10

Just as teaching is always evolving, so is management. People are coming up with new ideas all the time. You may think there's an area that this book doesn't cover but which is important to your situation. Write ten tips about a new area on page 198.

Section 1: Getting started

If you are reading this book, it is because you are interested in, or already involved in, managing some sort of language school, centre or department. Managing is one of the most difficult concepts to define because so much depends on the context and sector in which you are doing it. Levels of responsibility can vary enormously depending on the structure you are working in. There are aspects of leadership, stewardship and administration in most management positions, and in this book we hope to show you how to manage in a wide range of situations. Essentially, you can achieve this by doing what is expected of the manager: understanding, analysing, deciding, communicating and carrying out.

Everything we cover depends on your having a good basic understanding of what it takes to manage and what skills you already have. If you have managed before, you will already have views on what is involved in managing and leading people. In the first part of this section (Units 1 and 2) we look at the basics of what you need to know about management, and then go on to look at how managers are perceived in most language training contexts.

If you are thinking of moving into management, or who just want to consolidate what you have already learnt, you will find support in Units 3 and 4, which describe the industry standards and the different types of structure you might find yourself in. As a teacher you will have been put in situations where a lot of interpersonal skills are needed; Unit 5 looks at how you can use some of the skills you already have in a leadership role. You will not be able to develop fully without external support, and so Unit 6 offers ideas on where you can get this help. The section ends by looking at the kinds of conversations that should be taking place in your school if you are going to be able to manage successfully.

10 things you need to know about management

If you're a language teacher looking to make the move into ELT management, or someone thinking about applying for a position with management responsibilities in a language school, there are a number of things worth remembering. They will help you cope with the inevitable moments when you face a problem you weren't expecting. They will also help you realise the positive aspects of leading and managing a team of people in a language school.

1. It is very rewarding

Leading a group of people and managing any sort of project is a valuable experience for anyone. Being faced with a problem, discussing solutions with a number of people, deciding what to do and carrying it out is very satisfying. Being able to combine your experience and intuition with those of others and come to a conclusion that will improve the quality of service in the classroom or help learning conditions get better is one of the most rewarding outcomes of a manager's job.

2. Everyone needs training

A lot of people are reluctant to take on responsibility because they lack confidence in certain skills, whether that relates to IT, logistics, health and safety, teacher training or other administrative or pedagogic matters. The myth here is that certain people have all this knowledge and take to management very smoothly. The truth is that nearly every management position will involve skills that a new manager will require training in. There will be systems to learn, processes to use (and question), and styles to follow. There might be particular meetings to attend and relationships to maintain for which you will require help and coaching. Don't expect to do it alone and don't be afraid to ask for help.

3. Be a good communicator

One thing you learn very early on as a teacher is the need to communicate clearly and in good time, so that your students are always as well informed as they can be. Collaboration with other teachers, team-teaching and peer observations are all opportunities to improve this skill, so that when you are in a position of responsibility, you can keep your colleagues fully informed in a timely, unambiguous way. A common mistake made by managers is not informing the right people at the right time, which can lead to difficulties in the staffroom. Learn to be consistent in what you say and who you say it to, and also learn to know when to keep quiet. Until a decision has been made, don't fall into the trap of speaking too soon.

4. Be decisive

The people who put you in the position of manager expect action. There will be decisions to make, often ones that should have been made already. Weigh up the options, evaluate them, listen to an appropriate number of people and then make your decision. It is always better to be decisive (even if you don't get it quite right) than to dither. Once the decision has been made, stick with it, amend it and, if absolutely necessary, abandon it if it proves to be the wrong one.

5. Be consistent

One of the hardest skills to develop is consistency, simply because no situation is ever the same. Teachers and learners vary tremendously with a wide range of personality types, learning and teaching styles and academic expectations. Judgements you make, opinions you offer and steps you choose to take have to be consistent so that staff and customers can have confidence in you.

6. Read about it

Everyone needs to keep learning how to manage. One readily available way of getting ideas is to read about it. Blogs, articles and book reviews are everywhere, and they usually offer ideas to consider. As with any form of professional development, it is a good idea to make small changes and see how they work, rather than to radically alter your style. By keeping a regular eye on what is being suggested for managers in other areas of business, as well as in ELT, you can pick up lots of useful tips on how to manage your time, how to have tricky conversations, how to deal with data, etc. Before you attend an interview for a position, it is useful to read up a little. In that way, you will be able to show that you are interested in embracing new ideas.

7. Get a mentor

It might not happen automatically, but it is really useful to have a mentor when you first take on management responsibilities. You might need to choose one yourself, but this is no bad thing. The mentor could be a manager above you or perhaps the owner of the school; they could even be someone who doesn't work in your organisation ¬– in fact, sometimes this is a bonus. Whether or not the mentor works in your organisation, they should be there to listen to you, support you and guide you. They are not there to tell you what to do. Having a mentor allows you to talk off the record and be listened to in a non-judgemental way, allowing you more creative space to come up with good solutions.

8. Don't expect immediate approval

It can be quite hard at first when the people you are managing don't appear to be hugely positive about you and your decisions. It is a difficult job with a steep learning curve, and people are going to wait and see how you do. Ironically, if you are doing well, they probably won't tell you. Just be patient. You will probably win them over in the end. Don't forget, many people you manage don't want to manage themselves; indeed, they might already have tried it and not got on with it.

9. Manage your time

It's very easy to spend too long at work in a new position of responsibility. You will be busy doing the job itself and you will also want to spend time getting up to speed on aspects you are less confident about. Beware of letting your work hours expand too much into your private time. Becoming a manager does not mean losing the right to a life outside work. Keep that work-life balance healthy. Most successful managers are adept at getting others to help. When we first start managing, we don't want to appear too needy or too bossy; however most people are happy to help, so make sure you ask them. Once you have delegated a task, be sure to show that you are interested in how things are going, but beware of 'micromanaging' (i.e. being too involved).

10. Reflect

Effective managers are also reflective. They develop the ability to draw on their experiences and learn from their mistakes. If you are considering becoming a manager, try this activity: think about the points above in relation to how you currently manage your classes and teaching load. Order them from 1 to 9 in terms of how ready you feel you are to take on more responsibility. Which ones are going to require the most effort on your part?

"If you are successful at persuading, encouraging, motivating and keeping on track your students then many of the skills you employ will be suited to management. People-skills are very important in leading staff and management uses many of these skills that you will have been utilising and developing as a teacher. Great teachers don't need to shout and bully their students and it's the same with great managers."

Duncan Perrin, Manager Strategic Projects and Teacher Development, Monash University English Language Centre, Melbourne, Australia

10 misconceptions people have about managers

Management is something everyone does on a personal level every day. Planning, organising, choosing, setting deadlines, making decisions and controlling budgets are things that every adult has to do. In an educational institute, teachers have a huge amount of management to do in terms of goal-setting, planning, delegating, resourcing, problem-solving, etc. So in many ways teachers are getting lots of management training just by doing their job. But there still seems to be some reluctance to become a manager. Let's begin by looking at some negative perceptions of managers and try to view them in a more positive light.

1. **Managers often think of the organisation before the individual**

    It is often said that managers cannot afford to consider individual opinions if those opinions interfere with the direction the organisation is going. Yet if you think about good managers you have worked with, one of their strengths is the ability to deal with people on a personal basis while at the same time moving the team forward in the direction the general strategy requires. To achieve this you will need to develop the capacity to show each person how they fit into the overall plans for the organisation as well as how they will continue to develop as individuals.

2. **They don't always express their own opinions**

    Managers are often placed in a position where they have to speak on behalf of the organisation rather than expressing their own opinion. This is particularly difficult when the manager has been promoted from within the staff. The newly promoted manager will be open to criticism for apparently abandoning their principles (or 'selling out'). For example, as a manager, you might be asked to oversee aspects of a system that you personally disagree with. It is worth persevering, though, because it will happen quite often and these occurrences can usually be turned into useful learning experiences. Remember to choose carefully between voicing your own opinion and that of the role you are filling.

3. **They are out of touch with reality**

    Moving out of the classroom for even a few hours a week changes the perspective of the teacher/manager in terms of how they view the students and their learning. When a teacher is responsible for their own classes, they have an in-depth knowledge of the students, the curriculum, the content, and so on. A manager, on the other hand, has a 'helicopter view', looking at the bigger picture across a number of classes. Managers obtain the information they need by reading teachers' class records and reports. For them, every individual student is important, but so too are the courses and policies that relate to all students. Be aware of the different sources you will need to use to keep abreast of what is happening in your classrooms.

4. They only comment on negative feedback

Unlike the majority of teachers, managers tend to have most dealings with students who are either unhappy or underperforming. As such, a key management skill involves dealing positively with dissatisfaction. Get used to talking to staff on a regular basis and knowing what they are doing. In that way, any necessary feedback can be communicated in a reasonable, non-threatening way. Ensure also that good feedback does get passed on to teachers by setting up processes that circulate all feedback on a regular basis. Feedback should not be restricted to the teaching staff, either. All staff who regularly interact with students need to be kept informed of how their dealings are being perceived, and how they are adding value to the service being offered.

5. They are more interested in processes than performance

Schools are judged on their ability to help their students along their journey. A Business English student might be sent by their employer for an hour of private language tuition every week for a few months to improve their ability to communicate in English. Or a family might send their 18 year old to an English-speaking country for a foundation course to make them better prepared for the academic world. At every stage of these journeys there are choices to consider, key decisions to be made, options to evaluate, advice to be offered and assessments to be carried out – and all of these events need to be recorded. Overseeing these processes is a key part of management, but that does not mean that there is no room for intuition, risk-taking or trusting your own judgement. Use the systems to complement your judgement.

6. They are good at administration but less good with people

It is often said that good teachers have the interpersonal skills required of any manager. This is true, but as we have already said, administration has become a major part of management. Systems are set up which have to be adhered to, processes are in place for everything from recruitment to dealing with difficult customers. Accreditation is often achieved as much by the procedures in place as by the people carrying out those procedures. Make sure that as a manager you use those systems, even when you feel they are not that efficient. You have time to evaluate and make suggestions on how they could be improved, but in the meantime use what is there. Prove to everyone that you are as good with systems as you are with people.

7. They don't take suggestions on board

One thing that is often complained about in language schools is that there are some obvious areas for change that the management seem loath to consider. This might be an overcomplicated testing procedure or a timetabling system that creates more problems than it solves. Whatever the issue, make sure that, as a manager, you listen to suggestions and make it clear which ones are being adopted, which ones are not, and for what reason. Not all suggestions can be taken on board, but good managers acknowledge good suggestions and where they have come from.

8. **They aren't around**
    Managers who encourage independence and decisiveness can be accused of not being around enough. On the other hand, there are also managers who are accused of being around too much! This can be particularly tricky if you are the only person being managed. In many ways it is better to be one of a number of direct reports so you have more space. Part of the natural evolution of a manager is wanting to nurture talent and, ideally, see that talent develop as far as it can. Make sure you give your reports space to act and develop – plan catch-up meetings to allow them time to report on their progress and to ask for advice.

9. **They don't listen**
    One of the most frequently heard criticisms of managers is their inability to listen, or at least their inability to listen and act. Unfortunately, they cannot always act in the ways desired, but they should make every effort to make that clear as they listen. Active listening is a key attribute of modern managers; few of us do it naturally, so it is a skill that has to be learnt. Remember that being able to really listen to a member of staff can be vital in ensuring that the people you manage feel trusted and able to trust you.

10. **They have favourites**
    Managers have to be seen to be fair, and this fairness spreads as far as spending equal amounts of time with staff. There will always be people with whom a manager has more empathy or shares interests, but it is vital that all members of staff get time to discuss their classes, any suggestions they may have, or something they need to get off their chest.

10 areas of management in ELT

ELT managers are in a particularly unique position in that the areas of responsibility in ELT are very far-ranging. One day you might be enrolling new students, the next you're analysing feedback or checking copy for a new brochure. This can be either motivating or overwhelming, depending on the circumstances. However, you are likely to find that certain areas allow you to play to your strengths whereas others will require you to seek training and hard work to get you up to scratch. Here's an introductory list of ten key areas in ELT management that will be expanded upon in later units.

1. Operations and logistics

This is one of the areas where an ability to deal with data is useful. For a lot of people, coming into language teaching from an arts and languages background can initially come as a bit of a shock, but most people eventually find it an interesting part of the job. A lot of what is required from you will depend on context: are you sending teachers to teach off-site? Are you receiving inbound students via airports and bus transfers? Are you timetabling a large number of classes into a finite set of classrooms? Whatever the operational task, organisation of information is usually the key. Make sure you have everything you need to know or, at least know where and when you can get it.

2. Human resources (HR)

One of the main areas of HR that you will be involved in is recruitment. This will mean dealing with applications as well as interviewing and task-setting. It will also involve mentoring and offering in-service training to staff. HR-related work might also lead you into areas where difficult conversations are needed to discuss performance and other issues. You will need to have a good handle on employment law, and this might be one area where your personal opinion and the policies of your employer might be slightly different. For example, zero-hour and casual contracts have become commonplace in the training sector, and this might be something you are not comfortable with despite it being both legal and widely practised. Remember to retain objectivity in all HR-related conversations.

3. Product development

Markets and customers are constantly changing, and many successful suppliers react to these changes in terms of the products they offer. It is advisable to keep real data relating to your courses and to analyse the information closely to see what trends are being revealed. How popular are the courses? What results are participants getting from them? Is the content still reliable and useful? The more you analyse, the more you will be able to tweak, alter or replace products. Keeping an eye on the competition will also give you invaluable data. What products are growing? How are they being marketed? What materials are being used? We look at this area more closely in Units 21 and 23.

4. Marketing

Whatever your role in the institution, you are likely to be involved in marketing its products. Teachers are directly involved as they are dealing with some of your best opinion leaders – their classes. Word of mouth is a hugely important aspect of marketing, particularly since there are so many ways of recommending or complaining via social media. Networking has always been an important means of marketing services, and the benefits of visiting agents and potential contacts, as well as receiving them as guests at the school and explaining to them what you can offer, are many. Talking about the reality of what goes on in the classroom, how a new programme could be constructed and what resources would be used are areas where managers who have recent classroom experience are in high demand. Learning how to talk about those things from this slightly different perspective is a skill you will develop.

5. Professional development

One of the first steps people often take in terms of academic management is the role of mentor or senior teacher to one teacher or a group of teachers. This is usually a good way of finding out how well suited you are to teacher training and teacher development. Encouraging staff to develop is a long-term plan for all good institutions, and getting the right balance of introducing new approaches and maintaining standards is vital. As part of the academic management team, you might find yourself encouraging colleagues to lead or attend sessions, present at conferences, take further qualifications or think about taking on new responsibilities. A background in teacher training will be useful for this sort of role but is not compulsory. All of these areas require the manager to demonstrate sensitivity, active listening skills and a genuine interest in people.

6. Systems

No language teaching organisation can survive without good systems for enrolling, managing and recording the progress of the students they are teaching. All systems rely on staff inputting the information correctly, and these tasks can become quite mundane. Without such records, however, teaching and learning cannot be properly assessed. Despite increases in the speed and memory size of computers, there never seems to be much of a drop in the amount of time managers spend recording and analysing data; it looks likely to continue to be a major part of the academic manager's role for the foreseeable future.

7. Customer service

The most important part of any school is the student body, and that is why the way we deal with students is critical for maintaining a good level of teaching and learning. What good service really boils down to is respect for the customer, rather than a blind following of the 'customer is king' mantra. Ensure a good level of service by making sure that clients are getting what they expect, that the learning conditions and other services are as good as possible, and that students are genuinely listened to when they offer feedback.

8. Compliance

'Compliance' means ensuring that everything the institution does follows local laws, regulations and policies. One particularly important area is data protection; this is especially significant when you are dealing with large numbers of enrolments containing a lot of personal data. As a manager you will have to ensure that areas you are responsible for are compliant with local regulations. This could mean carrying out certain checks on teachers' backgrounds, ensuring your assessment methods follow the correct procedures, or monitoring attendance from students whose visa approval is dependent on being in class. Finally, you will need to be aware of any local regulations relating to your school's accreditation requirements.

9. Finance

Academic management will always involve certain activities linked to finance. This involvement might be on a very basic level, such as buying resources, paying for subscriptions, or ensuring that a budget does not overrun. Another aspect of finance-related activity might be getting the class sizes right, based on both pedagogic and financial criteria. Institutions will not be able to afford classes that drop below the expected income levels, and opening a new class can have a considerable impact on profitability. You will have to learn about key performance indicators for your institution, such as average class size, ratio of teaching costs to income, and average cost per student for teaching materials (including photocopies and copyright protection fees). An understanding of these elements will greatly improve your ability to manage a successful school.

10. Performance

Another important part of the manager's role is to monitor and improve performance. A language teaching institution has to improve the learners' ability to use the language in as efficient, engaging and enduring a way as possible. Of course, this puts a lot of pressure on the teachers, but there are other elements within the school that also need to perform well: technology, self-study systems, assessment methods and support staff. As well as making sure average performance on an average day is good, managers also need to ensure that everyone can improve within their own context and style. Keep in mind, too, that improving performance which is already good is just as important as training up those who are underperforming.

Think about the school where you are currently working. If you were to do a performance rating today, which areas would require the most improvement? Make a list of key areas and reflect on how they might be improved.

10 roles and responsibilities in an ideal management team

Most institutions over a certain size have a team of managers whose combined responsibilities cover the whole learner journey from the initial enquiry right through to course completion. Being part of a team has the benefit of removing a lot of pressure from individuals; it also ensures that most people can play to their strengths. In an ideal world this adds up to a very positive learning experience for all members of the team. In larger institutions there will be a wide range of senior management roles helping to develop the vision and strategy. In this unit we will concentrate on the roles and responsibilities of the hands-on operational team.

1. Organising and monitoring learning

The academic manager is responsible for organising and monitoring students' learning. They take into consideration each student's learning objectives, their current level and the amount of time they have available. They will also try to choose the most suitable class and teacher, and monitor progress regularly, either through student and teacher feedback, by sitting in on classes or through informal conversations with participants and teachers.

2. Timetabling

At the heart of all institutions is the timetable. A wide range of factors have to be taken into consideration when deciding which teachers will teach which classes in which rooms. If the teaching is to be taking place off-site, the teacher's journey from their home to the teaching location will also need to be considered. Long working days are illegal in certain countries, whether that relates to the number of teaching hours in total or the span of the day from the first class to the last. Trying to ensure that each class is taught well with each teacher having a good spread of classes can be further complicated by teacher preferences for level and the need to continually vary their load. Timetabling requires more than just a good knowledge of spreadsheets: knowing the teachers and the students is also key. It is also an excellent way of developing a wide range of management skills and handling both qualitative and quantitative data. (See also Unit 35.)

3. Assessing students for level

Being responsible for assessing learners' levels is an important role for both pedagogic and commercial reasons. All learners are usually assessed and placed in the appropriate level of class when they first join an institution. Stakeholders in this placement include the learner, future classmates, parents, and anyone else interested in the progress made by the learner. Although initial placement is important, it is only a judgement call based on test materials, level descriptors and the assessor's experience and intuition. If the learner is further ahead or further behind than at first realised, then a change can be made. A level co-ordinator's role might involve choosing appropriate materials and coursebooks for the level, advising on curriculum and assessing progress. Depending on your school, there might be specific language areas to be assessed, including grammar, vocabulary, pronunciation, and the four main skills as well as soft skills, such as collaboration and communication.

4. Welfare and student advice

There are numerous factors outside the classroom that can have an impact on learners, and many of these come under the remit of the student counsellor. Typical areas of concern will vary depending on the age of the learner, the nature of the course and its location. Learners outside their home country may have intercultural issues to contend with, a new teaching approach, or psychological matters linked to being away from home. All students will be concerned about the amount of progress they are making and will feel under pressure if expectations (theirs and those of other stakeholders) are not being met. Many students have no real understanding of the amount of time and effort required to make progress in a language, which relies so much on practice and skills development.

5. Sales and marketing

In many institutions, particularly smaller ones, sales and marketing are the responsibility of the same people. Teachers often move into these areas because there are transferable skills involved: good teachers are usually quite persuasive, articulate and good at communicating, and so are good salespeople. Knowing exactly what goes on in the classroom and how challenges can be overcome is a useful attribute when promoting a particular institution or course. Writing honest but engaging promotional materials or social media content can also come more easily to people who have recently been teaching because they have recent practical examples to base their claims on. There are excellent sales and marketing people who haven't come from the classroom, but it really can be a plus if teaching experience can be tapped into. For those who come from a non-teaching background, ensure they have an active observation role within the school. As non-experts, they will have worthwhile comments to make about the teaching being delivered. Likewise, encourage managers who have come from an academic background to sit in on sales or finance meetings.

6. Curriculum and course design

This is an area that is key to an institution's success and needs careful and constant management. Most learners will only experience a part of the curriculum, as they will only be in the school for a fixed period of time but it is vital that each part is well paced, varied and meaningful with realistic and achievable learning outcomes. Institutions offering short, intensive courses might only be able to focus on one or two skills or prepare a learner for a particular exam or a professional task like a conference or a presentation; however, whatever the time available, appropriate aims and course content should be provided. In institutions where the learners attend classes for longer periods, the curriculum has to be graded and paced to cover a reasonable amount of learning – not so much that it becomes overwhelming and difficult, but not so little that learners feel they are coasting.

7. Product research and development

We have already mentioned that, as the market changes, institutions need to reassess their courses and develop new ones. Schools make huge efforts to take advantage of new technologies in language teaching in order to develop independent study through blended learning and flipped classrooms. And this will continue to become increasingly important as learners insist on getting maximum benefit from their courses. Make sure that the investment your school makes in new technology is well considered and future-proofed. This makes the role of course research and design increasingly important.

8. Recruitment

Having the right staff ensures that the majority of courses delivered will be well designed, successfully marketed, professionally delivered and accurately assessed. Getting the right people and keeping them is therefore key. Choosing staff who are going to fit in, who are going to bring something new and who are also going to want to stay for a reasonable length of time comes down to having good recruitment systems in place and a reputation for being a good employer. Having the best possible terms available will always act in the institution's interests as they try to attract good staff, but there are other factors which can help with recruitment, such as good professional development and career opportunities. See Unit 15 for more on this.

9. In-service training

One factor that is usually high on the list of what staff expect from an employer is good-quality training. It seems logical that an organisation dedicated to teaching would consider education for their own staff as a priority, but this is not always the case. Organisations that take training seriously and provide just enough in-service training tend to retain and develop good teachers. Getting it right is hard since some teachers do not welcome extra training, seeing themselves as already adequately qualified. Others might require more training, so coming up with a training plan which is the result of talking to the staff is an important management decision. Finally, ensure that your organisation is offering a wide range of delivery methods such as workshops, meetings, subscriptions to magazines and attendance at conferences.

10. Learner technology and resources

We touched earlier on the importance of technology in teaching. Management of those resources is a vital part of the management team's responsibilities. There are a huge number of decisions to be made to make sure the best possible learning environment is being set up. Sometimes the key decision might already have been made regarding which learning platform to use, for example. For the person responsible for this area, however, there is still much to do. Finding a balance of useful, efficient and trackable learning activities which appeal to both learners and teachers is what this role is all about.

Spend some time thinking about your current school. What technology resources are available to your teachers and students? Could there be more? Would they be used? How would things have to change?

10 transferable skills for teachers who want to be managers

Becoming a manager should not be seen as a major change, but rather part of normal career development. Taking on new responsibilities might involve managing other teachers, but it might also mean managing projects, resources, students or a mixed team of both teachers and administrative staff. There are plenty of skills that you will have developed in the classroom and which are going to be of immediate use in your new role. This unit will allow you to identify which ones you have already.

1. Communication

Language training is fundamentally about developing your students' communicative ability, and as a teacher you are well versed in the importance of these skills and how to use them effectively. You need to present new language and content, keep your classes informed about their development, have tutorials and other conversations, listen actively to their worries and suggestions and report concisely and unambiguously on their progress. As soon as you take on a management role, you will need to be able to move projects forward and hold meetings to inform people of your decisions, always remembering to listen to people and to let them know their views have been taken on board. Many of these skills have been honed in the classroom and can be transferred to a managerial role.

2. Product development

As a teacher, you might well have developed an interest in course design and materials development. It might have been for class use only, for example, a worksheet to sit alongside a reading text or a game to provide revision of a particular item. You might have been involved in organising teaching hours to fit a new coursebook or writing assessments for a particular level. As a user of classroom resources and the main driver of progress for a particular class, you are in an excellent position to use that know-how on a broader level for other classes apart from your own. The knowledge you have about curriculum design for one class now needs to be broadened to cover a number of classes. Similarly, your ability to produce materials for one or two classes will be useful across the whole school.

3. Project management

Managing any group of learners for the duration of a course and achieving the expected learning outcomes requires great skill. Keeping all the students engaged and interested, however well they are doing, and making sure that their individual milestones are being met is just one example of project management. Ensuring learners, parents, sponsors and managers are all informed of progress, have opportunities to give feedback and know that they will be listened to is all part of this process. Getting any group of learners from A to B given all the variables there will be on the way is a great testament to your project management skills.

4. Training and professional development

As you reflect on your own teaching, perhaps carrying out small classroom research projects, you will gain a valuable insight into how students learn. Making small adjustments to your practice and seeing what happens is a rewarding way of developing your own good practice. Reading and peer observations will add to your understanding, as will developing a working knowledge of the teaching materials available. An academic management role in any school or department would require this sort of experience. It will put you in good stead to lead workshops, observe teachers and be of use on the professional development team.

5. Course design and curriculum

Experience you have gained in the classroom will give you a head start when it comes to helping with course development and curriculum design. Your institution might perceive a gap in the market or a new type of student and want to encourage them to sign up. To do this successfully, the organisation has to be able to offer a course designed with appropriate aims and objectives, and a clear prediction of the time required. Your skills will be valuable in ensuring that the learning outcomes, success criteria and course content are coherent. At a later stage you might develop into a materials writer, briefed to ensure that the institution's resources remain up to date and relevant.

6. Assessment

'Assessment literacy' (i.e. understanding how assessment can be used to inform our teaching as well as how it can inform students about their achievements) is a major part of professional development in many institutions. Developing assessment materials that are both valid and efficient (in terms of time spent) is a skill only a small number of teachers are likely to have. As the language-learning world becomes more used to detailed level descriptors, and a requirement to prove the reliability of assessment tools becomes the norm, teachers with skills in assessment will be valuable and in high demand.

7. Mentoring

Mentoring is usually carried out by more experienced teachers in a school, and is an excellent learning experience for a senior teacher on the way to becoming a manager. The skills required of a good mentor are an ability to listen, to offer useful, practical, immediate solutions, to reassure, and to provide a sympathetic ear. While a mentor usually has only a couple of mentees and has to leave certain questions for the managers to answer, even on this reduced scale, mentoring constitutes very useful preparation for certain management techniques.

8. Promotion

One adjective that often features in positive student evaluations is 'enthusiastic'. Teachers who show enthusiasm tend to be well respected by learners. This passion can manifest itself in different ways, but learners are sensitive to it and teachers and managers need to develop it if they haven't got it. It is hard to be enthusiastic all the time, but it is important for teachers to remember that, although they might be covering a particular language item for the hundredth time, it is not the hundredth time for the learner. This ability to kindle interest at any time of the week or term is a huge asset, and can be transferred into a sales or marketing role. Clients often respond positively to an enthusiastic person, and combined with trust, the result can be a persuasive combination.

9. Versatility

When we talk about ELT management, 'versatility' is a word that often crops up. Managers need to be great generalists who can cope with a wide range of tasks, tapping into a large skill set. Making sure classrooms are fit for purpose might well involve moving furniture one minute and the next you might be showing a potential customer around the same building. You could be checking attendance for visa purposes in the morning and trying to give helpful feedback to one of your teachers in the afternoon. This versatility is often gained from teaching, where you are often called upon to perform professionally in a rapidly changing situation.

10. Classroom management in general

All the tasks performed in a classroom have their management equivalents. Spend some time looking at a typical day and deciding what management hats a teacher has on at any given time, from checking attendance, to dealing with latecomers, to setting up tasks, to giving instructions, and so on. Look at the table on page 160 of the Appendix and discuss with colleagues or reflect alone on which skills you have which are transferable.

> *"Moving from teaching to management presents its challenges, but there are many transferable skills and approaches that can stand a teacher in good stead. Time and workload management, organisational skills, and coping with complexity will all be familiar. The teacher's people skills with individuals and across teams, as well as the self-awareness that develops from self-reflective teaching, and the ability to make reasoned judgements are transferable directly to the management office. Perhaps most important however, is that unique insight teachers have into what is of most relevance to successful teaching and learning, that can be positively influenced when they move into a management role."*
>
> **Jo Thomas, Centre Director Centre for Languages, Wintec, Hamilton, New Zealand**

10 external organisations and partners you need to work with

It is nice to think of a language school existing in isolation with a fixed number of teachers and happy, motivated students. This would mean an easier teaching environment, more homogeneous classes and time to focus on teaching your class. In reality, schools are in a constant state of flux, with new learners to get started, established classes heading towards the end of a term, short courses coming and going, exam classes getting close to deadlines and so on. The world outside the school is also changing, and a lot of those changes will bring benefits or challenges to the school. To be in the best place to deal with them all is to be in regular contact with other external organisations.

1. **Teachers' associations**

   Every country, region and town has associations of teachers, formed with the aim of sharing ideas, discussing issues and helping to professionalise the industry. Encouraging staff to attend meetings and conferences, and joining local teachers' associations yourself, will keep your institution in touch with what is happening in terms of the market, the law, national or regional policies, and innovations in course content and delivery.

2. **Providers' associations**

   These are groups of schools with similar aims and values. There may well be a mix of private and public organisations within the association, but they will all be keen to share ideas and discuss issues, particularly in terms of large data and trends. Talking to competitors allows you to see which sectors are growing and which are in decline, and might even provide you with good sources of potential staff members if you can offer career opportunities to new recruits. Associations often have more influence compared with individual organisations, so membership is nearly always beneficial. At all levels, lobbying by groups will have a bigger impact than that done by an individual, whether in terms of improving standards, developing the profession, or speaking up for a particular sector on a specific issue such as health and safety.

3. **ELT publishers**

   It's worth forming a relationship with both local publishers and international publishers. The larger publishers are keen to involve schools and institutions in market research, and this can be an interesting area for certain teachers to get involved in. Helping with research might sometimes lead to other work, such as writing materials or helping promote titles at conferences. Publishers are also aware of the kinds of courses that are being developed elsewhere, giving you a broader view of the ELT world. Their websites and teachers' clubs also provide a huge amount of professional development and teaching resources.

4. **Government ministries and associations**

   The extent to which you are involved with ministries and government organisations will depend on the status of your school and the type of learner you are dealing with. In many countries, the ministry of education (or equivalent) has a lot of influence over curriculum, learning outcomes and assessment, and it is beneficial for organisations to be a part of that consultation process. In other countries, organisations such as the British Council have an important role to play and can be a useful source of advice and ideas.

5. Examination boards

The influence of examination boards on ELT continues to grow as their exams are used as proof of level for an increasing range of activities – from university entry through to visa applications. With so many students learning with a view to working, studying or living in an English-speaking context, exams like TOEFL, TOEIC or IELTS have become ends in themselves for certain students. Knowing what the exam boards are doing and planning is therefore important. Encouraging teachers to become examiners or item writers is a useful part of professional development.

6. Influencers

As in any industry, there are various influencers you might need to be aware of. Everyone is looking for the next 'magic method' that can be used to teach anyone English quickly. Speakers at conferences, bloggers, marketing experts and researchers will all claim to have discovered something new. New teaching approaches come and go; some have a short life but others can have an influence on your teachers and learners. With the development of social media, these influencers can have an impact more quickly than in the past. In any case, all new ideas are worth knowing about and evaluating. Most classes and teachers rely on a combination of approaches and methods developed over time. Learner-centered teaching, for example, should be a key aspect of your classes but not 100% of the time. Other approaches that demand high levels of pronunciation or grammatical accuracy are equally valid, but if you have only three hours a week and a full curriculum, compromises will have to be made. As with so many aspects of management, you will need to evaluate what is out there and make a call as to what your institution should take on board.

7. Agents

If you are working in a market where schools benefit from recommendations and sales from third-party agents, you will be aware of how important it is to remain in regular contact with them and their associations. As well as being a valuable source of customers in their own right, they can be very useful in suggesting new course types for you to consider offering.

8. Accreditation bodies

Depending on your market, there will be various bodies offering accreditation. The benefits of being accredited include being compliant with national requirements, being benchmarked to a particular standard, and being validated in a way that will allow you to attract both customers and staff. The downside of the process is that the actual inspection can put a lot of stress on your organisation at a busy time of the year. Once the right systems and processes are in place, however, it should allow your organisation to run more efficiently, so it is worth ensuring those standards are always maintained. Not being accredited in a market where the competition does have accreditation will make your commercial survival difficult. Try to ensure that the criteria used to benchmark the various aspects of the organisation at inspection time are also used at other times as part of an ongoing quality improvement process.

9. Consumers

Language teaching is just like any other product in that there are consumer organisations testing and commenting on our products and services – and rightly so. Huge amounts of money are invested by governments, companies, parents and individuals in an attempt to improve language levels, and all customers are entitled to a reasonable return, good learning conditions, qualified teachers, realistic aims and excellent resources. We know what we would expect as end users, and we must ensure our customers get the same.

10. Local business support and training organisations

It is always good to step outside the bubble of our own school and even outside the ELT industry itself to connect with other local organisations. Language learning is not really understood by most people, other than the fact that it is difficult, so any chance to network and promote your organisation should not be ignored. Local firms thinking about investing in language training will approach the people they know, so try to raise your organisation's profile whenever you can. You will also find that the more you know about how other businesses and organisations are run, the more your own business will benefit.

Find out the following:

▶ How do other organisations find customers?

▶ How do they develop new products?

▶ How do they set their prices?

All sorts of information is available once you take the time to form relationships outside your immediate circle.

"The following partners stand out as milestones in the development of our school. Joining the International House World Organisation back in the 80s provided expertise in teacher training, recruitment and methodology. Then working for and obtaining accreditation with the EAQUALS Association in the 90s helped enormously to improve our systems of work and later with the incorporation of the CEFR system of levels. I have no doubt that the school would not have developed so successfully without the contribution these external organisations have made and, in fact, continue to make."

John Bradley – Ex IH San Sebastian]

10 conversations that need to happen in your school

Some of the best managers are those who are good at MWA (Managing by Walking Around). The benefits of talking to people both in and around your institution cannot be overstated. These conversations should take place regularly so that the exchange becomes natural and honest: everyone will gain from the chance to run their niggles, ideas and suggestions past you. By listening and showing that you find these conversations valuable, you will gain a lot of useful information. As with any strategy, use with care. Staff are not keen to be continually interrupted by a manager striving to be communicative. The conversations below are examples of when and how this approach can be used in a positive way.

1. How's it going?

The most important conversation of the day for many people is that brief chat on arrival, particularly if you can use it to find out how they are and what is happening. Make sure you know what levels people are teaching, what projects they are working on, if there is a new student in the class or if there is an exam coming up. Having your finger on the pulse in this way will allow colleagues to share things with you. It also prevents small things becoming blown out of all proportion. Maybe a room can be changed or a meeting shortened; perhaps some help with marking can be offered or a standby teacher found: any of these things might well just ease the pressure on a teacher. You can only find out what they need, though, by having regular chats and being approachable.

2. How did it go?

Equally important is knowing when people have been trying out something new, dealing with a difficulty or simply dealing with an extra task like an observation or a parents' meeting. Afterwards, allow them to give you some feedback, let off steam or even congratulate themselves. You can make sure that happens by simply being around to ask the question.

3. Well done!

Most of us like to be recognised for our successes, and nothing is more motivating than being praised unexpectedly, particularly by someone who has a million other things to think about. In any management position it is well worth being aware of the good things that people are doing and being ready to let them know. Comments such as 'I hear your class did really well with their project work' or 'Thanks for covering that class last week – the feedback was very good' are worth their weight in gold to a busy teacher.

4. Being around

Having an open-door attitude, even if you're in an open-plan office, is also a useful approach to management. Colleagues need to know that you are approachable and can be talked to. This is particularly important when you are in a new post or when you are dealing with new team members who need to get to know you. Being isolated and distant will not help. This doesn't mean you cannot have quiet times when you need to get on with other things. Just make sure you are available more often than not.

5. **Difficult conversations**

    Difficult conversations are a key part of any organisation. As a manager it is your role to ensure that all conversations are two-sided and that everyone is listened to and says what they want to say. Sometimes you will be passing judgement on someone, giving negative feedback or asking them to do something they don't want to do. Learn to do this in a neutral, natural and timely way. After a particularly difficult conversation, reflect on how it went, how the turns were taken, where it ended and how well it really went. Did all parties speak their minds? Did everyone understand the same things? Were your points clearly made and understood? Rehearse particularly sensitive conversations and try and predict how things might go.

6. **Appraisal conversations**

    These will make up a formal part of the employment terms but it is important that (a) they actually take place and (b) they are taken seriously. As one of the conversations that should be taking place in a well-managed organisation, they are crucial. Ensuring that people think about their goals and ambitions in a serious, structured way is something all good schools should do. We look at appraisals in more detail in Unit 39.

7. **Informal chats**

    The chat in the kitchen or by the vending machine is also part of the management process. Talking to people as they come in and out of work sessions, be it teaching or administrating, is a unique opportunity to touch base with them and see what is on their minds. Great ideas can come from these chats, and it is a useful way of finding out unofficially what their plans, thoughts, aims and worries are.

8. **Suggestions meetings**

    It is often said that innovation is at the heart of all successful businesses and organisations, so why are so few places open to suggestions? The oft-repeated phrase: 'We've always done it this way – that's what people expect' might keep some staff and customers happy but it won't last for ever. 'We tried that before and it didn't work' is equally frustrating to hear. Make sure you have a system in place for conversations about your products, processes and services. For example, it could be a regular lunchtime slot every few weeks which is dedicated to suggestions. Maybe prizes could be awarded for the best suggestions of the year. If you have an online forum for staff members, dedicate part of it to new suggestions and make sure it is well moderated. Having a clear process for suggesting and getting feedback on suggestions will always pay off.

9. **'Welcome' conversations**

    So many great organisations fail to welcome new staff and students physically, thereby failing to ensure that, on a purely human level, people feel part of the new place. A lot of this can be overcome if people are introduced and common ground is found between them. In this way, the new staff member or student starts to feel part of something. Making sure that new students meet students from other classes, and that they know who the support staff are is also important, particularly when the teaching is off-site, or when staff operate at different times of the day.

10. Motivational conversations

As a manager, you might not have particular students you teach and, as such, your relationship with them will be different from those they have with their teachers. You will be the voice of the organisation and your opinions and comments will carry more weight, both in and out of the school. Make sure you find time to have conversations with them about their progress, their homework and their ambitions. This will make them feel looked after, and it will also give you some real insights into how your organisation works and how it handles different customers' journeys. If you do enough of this it will become part of the institutional approach, and your team will start to do the same. Ensuring that learners feel they can open up to teachers is an important step in making them feel they are part of an ongoing learning process. Of course, there will be issues and setbacks, but doing this will also create a general sense of confidence that solutions can be found.

> *"I love the idea of 'One Minute Praisings' (Ken Blanchard). The DoS walks around and tries to catch her employees doing something good, which she then reinforces with immediate praise – perhaps adding a positive label which then acts as a self-fulfilling prophecy: For instance [during recess]: 'I love the way you just replied to that student in English. You are so committed and you set such a good example'. "*
>
> **Nick Michelioudakis, trainer and author, Athens, Greece.**

10 questions to ask about strategic management

Strategic management is about the bigger picture; it involves setting objectives and achieving the whole organisation's goals. It is important for all levels of management, even if they are not key players in defining that strategy. This is because long-term vision and planning, together with the provision of services and skills that are not directly concerned with teaching and learning, will make that product all the stronger. This unit asks questions and sets activities that will help the new manager build an understanding of what strategic management means in practical terms.

1. **Are you a manager or a leader?**

   The terms 'leader' and 'manager' are often used synonymously, but there is a difference. Management is a set of processes that keep an organisation functioning. The processes can include planning courses, setting budgets, recruiting staff, clarifying roles, observing teachers, measuring performance and problem-solving. Leadership, on the other hand, is about aligning people to a future vision, communicating that vision and providing motivation and inspiration. A good leader is not necessarily a good manager, and a good manager is not necessarily a good leader. In many schools the two roles are performed by the same person; in such cases it is important for that person to be aware of the different roles. Which are you: a good leader, a good manager, or both? Go to the activity on page 161 of the Appendix.

2. **Do you have a mission statement and a vision statement?**

   A mission statement defines the school's business, its objectives and its approach to reaching those objectives. A vision statement describes the desired future position of the school and any wider purpose it may have. While a mission statement describes what a company wants to do now, a vision statement is grander; it outlines what a company wants to be and what it wants to achieve in the future. There is no rule about the length of vision and mission statements, but it is probably most effective to keep them concise and to the point. Here is an example from Michigan State University English Language Center:

   Vision: To foster a culture of global openness.

   Mission: To empower international students to become full participants in the university community through excellent instruction in language, cultural awareness and study skills.

   Write a mission statement and a vision statement. Go to the activity on page 162 of the Appendix.

3. **How are vision and mission statements shared and developed?**

   Producing a mission and a vision statement is only the start. Ideally there will have been some consultation within the school when writing the statements, although this is not always the case. Even if there has been a dialogue, you cannot be sure everyone will be aware of it, especially if you often recruit short-term staff. Make the statements public: on wall displays, on websites, on document headers, in marketing materials, on school logos and in any corporate materials. Vision and mission statements are not necessarily going to stay the same for ever. At the very least they need to be reviewed, for example at annual strategic review meetings. But they could also be looked at and commented on at staff meetings – and don't forget to get the views of your students and your school agents.

4. **What are the different levels of management in your school?**

   There are several levels of management in most schools, even if in smaller organisations the roles are carried out by the same person. The levels are often described as strategic, tactical and operational:

   ▶ The strategic manager will often be the principal or department head. They are responsible for long-term strategic planning and key negotiations, and for establishing the vision and mission of the school.

   ▶ The tactical manager will often be the director of studies, subject leader or student services manager. They execute the strategy and are responsible for selecting appropriate means of achieving a strategic plan or objective (e.g. setting up a new course or offering enhanced welfare provision).

   ▶ Operational managers are responsible for planning and executing the routine day-to-day functions and activities of the school, such as setting the timetable, observing classes and delivering lessons. All teachers, and indeed all staff, could well be regarded as operational managers.

   Who are the strategic, tactical and operational managers in your school? Go to the activity on page 162 of the Appendix.

5. **What are the strengths and weaknesses of your school?**

   It is important to know what you are good at as an organisation and what you are not so good at. But seeing your strengths and weaknesses when you are in the middle of the operation yourself is not always easy. Take time to step outside the frame of your everyday operational roles and evaluate what you do. Think about how others see you. Ask your friends, ask your competitors, ask the people who send you students (agents, parents and businesses). Benchmark what you do against other similar schools and institutions. Use the criteria that are publicly available from the various accreditation schemes, even if you are not due an inspection.

6. **Have you done a SWOT analysis?**

   There is one simple management tool that you can apply: the SWOT analysis matrix. This can help you to identify your strengths and weaknesses. You can use it on your own or as part of a group activity. Get different sectors to do it: teachers, administrative staff, welfare staff, the marketing department, students – and then compare the results. There is an example for you to complete on page 164 of the Appendix.

7. **What are the external factors affecting your school?**

   Managers cannot control everything; there will always be external factors that you can do little about. Government regulation, demographic change, economic conditions, changing needs for English language: all of these are largely beyond your control (although that shouldn't stop you from campaigning for better conditions for your school). You should identify what these external factors are and work out how you can minimise any negative impact, or even use them to your advantage.

8. **Have you done a STEP analysis?**

    External factors affecting an organisation can be categorised as STEP factors, divided into Social, Technological, Economic and Political. A STEP matrix can help you to identify specific factors, and, as with the SWOT analysis matrix, you can use it to plan ways of dealing with the external factors, either using them for your advantage or to minimise their impact. There is an example for you to complete on page 165 of the Appendix.

9. **Can you afford it?**

    Working out the financial viability and profitability of any project is crucial, especially if the project is a large-scale strategic plan for future developments. For some new managers this is one of the biggest challenges as they may not have had to deal with this type of thing to such an extent when in less senior roles. Cost analysis, negotiating favourable rates and preparing to make adjustments are all skills that the strategic manager needs to employ. Remember that training in these areas of management is available and worth investing in.

10. **Are you thinking in the long term?**

    The day-to-day management that teachers and managers are involved in is very important for running a successful operation. However, to make strategic planning effective you have to step away from the immediate needs and challenges and look at the longer term. The best way to do this is to set objectives in time frames, such as a three-year or five-year plan with specific goals for each year (or each term).

    In order to create your own strategic plan, begin by asking three simple questions:

    1. Where are we now?
    2. Where are we going?
    3. How will we get there?

    Next, use the SWOT and STEP analyses that you carried out in Tips 6 and 8 to produce a five-year strategic plan for your school, or for a school that you know well. There are many templates for strategic plans available online. Alternatively, try your own, customised to the specific context and needs of your school.

10 ways to ensure an organisation is dynamic

We often talk about management 'structures', but structures are usually seen as static, immovable objects or systems: they can provide security and stability, but they can also restrict and confine. For many new managers in schools, the management structure and management culture can indeed seem impenetrable and appear to involve a different set of values and approaches with power at the centre and teachers creating dependency cultures beyond the management strata. It doesn't have to be that way. For an organisation to be dynamic and adaptable, the structures, systems and communication channels need to allow flexibility.

1. Is your management structure flexible?

There are many ways of categorising different organisational structures. In the world of ELT we tend to talk about 'flat' or 'hierarchical' management structures. A flat organisation has few or no levels of middle management; it tends to supervise employees less and increase their involvement in decision-making. A hierarchical organisation consists of different levels of authority in a vertical link between superior and subordinate levels. There is no right or wrong way to structure your management system, and both systems have advantages and disadvantages. Whatever your organisational structure is, it is important to ensure it is not static and rigid, but that it is flexible enough to encourage energy and ideas, and is capable of following them through.

2. Use your organogram

An organogram is one visual way to present your management structure, and at a glance it will indicate the type of management structure you have. The organogram should be something you can use actively, and will need regularly updating as structures (and staff) change. Make sure you draw the lines of communication and, if applicable, who reports to whom and who line-manages which members of staff. Indicate any teams you have within the structure, using colour to identify them. Experiment with different representations of your organisation; for example, turn the diagram upside down, use alternative designs such as bubbles or concentric circles and put different staff and stakeholders in the centre, not just the managers but teachers, students, and so on. It will help you think differently and more proactively about your way of working.

3. Welcome ideas

Most managers will say they have an 'open-door' policy, but what does that really mean? Of course you want to encourage contact, but it isn't practical to have people randomly sharing ideas with you at all hours of the day. Simply encouraging communication without any specific focus is not enough. Be proactive, for example, by holding one-off 'think-tank' meetings looking at a specific area, focus groups and 'blue-sky thinking' sessions. And don't forget to keep your ear to the ground by chatting to a member of staff while you are in the coffee-bar queue.

4. **Ensure cover and continuity**

   Taking an interest in each other's jobs is a sign of a healthy organisation. It is also essential in order to provide effective cover for illness or holidays, and to ensure there is continuity in all operational areas. In most schools, work levels for particular roles will fluctuate, for example enrolment at the start of the academic year, or finding homestay accommodation in the busy summer period for junior vacation courses. It is essential that there are people who can not only step in and share the workload, but also offer informed support and sympathy. Cross-training (learning the skills required to perform another role) and job-sharing should be a regular feature of the dynamic and adaptable workplace.

5. **Promote with a purpose**

   Promotion is a natural and positive feature of all dynamic organisations, but particularly in schools, where staff turnover can often be high. If a vacancy arises, think proactively about who should fill it. Don't necessarily go for the obvious choice, but think how you can use the appointment to perhaps change the way you do things, or even change the direction of the school. You could also take the opportunity to reward a particular member of staff, or to keep a good employee who you know is thinking of leaving. In all of this you need to be sure you have people in the right roles.

6. **Make sure communication is effective**

   For the ELT manager, communication is our stock-in-trade and we should, in theory, be communication experts. But are we in control of it? Some simple reminders can help us to be effective and productive: always remember communication is a two-way process: know the person you are talking to and build a receptive atmosphere. Keep the message clear and simple, use the techniques of our trade such as grading language and checking understanding, and don't forget that body language and facial expressions are forms of communication. Perhaps, above all, learn the value of listening.

7. **Communication conventions**

   From the start, establish a house style for your communication systems. A lot of organisations have style guides for their written documentation; these indicate spelling rules, layout guidelines and when to use a hyphen or an en-rule, for example. Similar behavourial protocols for actual communication exchanges would be even more useful and could be established during induction training; for example how to address senior staff, how to make your message clear and check understanding. There are no universally accepted rules for the what, the who and the how of communication, but if your organisation can establish such conventions, it will lead to greater efficiency and effectiveness.

8. Establish rules for digital communication

The need for communication conventions and guidelines on using all aspects of digital communication is becoming greater as the choice of systems and platforms grows. Added to this is the fact that the range of digital competences can vary enormously. Everyone needs to know what means of communication is required for different functions (e.g. completing registers and reports, recording action points from a meeting) and whether it is the most effective for each purpose. Training will be needed for all digital applications: do not assume everyone is familiar with the latest systems. Also, avoid change for the sake of change: new applications do not always improve efficiency.

9. Get an outside perspective

When you are at the heart of an organisation you sometimes don't see the bigger picture. Try to stand outside and look in: it's not easy, but it's worthwhile. If that doesn't work, then ask someone who is outside the core organisation: the gardener, a neighbour, a rival organisation or a homestay host (if you provide accommodation). You may get an interesting and unexpected perspective.

10. Think in terms of outcomes and objectives

Every organisation needs to have objectives in order to move forward effectively. One frequently used management tool is to set 'SMART' objectives. This acronym represents five criteria: goals should be specific, measurable, attainable, relevant, and time-based. For example, if you are planning to introduce a new course, you should be specific about the content, how much work it will involve, whether it is attainable and relevant to the needs of the students and abilities of the teachers, and when you intend to introduce it. There are some variations on these five criteria, such as 'agreed upon' and 'realistic'. One way of encouraging your staff to think proactively about objectives specific to your organisation is to get everyone to give their view of what SMART could stand for, or maybe come up with another acronym.

 Try using SMART for yourself: think of one specific objective that you are trying to achieve at the moment. Can you set SMART objectives?

10 ways to encourage team-building and team morale

The job of a manager is made easier if the people they are managing function as a team rather than a group of individuals. In teams people work together and have specific roles which, when combined, make the whole greater than the sum of its parts. But remember that teachers aren't always used to working in a team when they are actually teaching, and might need training in this area. In any case, teams do not just happen automatically: they have to be built, nurtured and monitored.

1. **Start from the word go**

   Introduce the concept of teamwork when recruiting. At interview, ask the candidate about any teamwork experience, not necessarily in a language school environment, and include it as a question to referees. Set team tasks in the interview and during early training, for example group lesson planning and problem solving. Make sure you've got a team player, not just a good employee. A good team player is reliable, a good communicator, prepared to do more than asked, able to adapt quickly and easily, and can demonstrate genuine commitment. Ask for specific examples of these skills and how they have been used in practice.

2. **Beware of round pegs in square holes**

   You might have a very good team player on your staff, but it's important to be sure they are capable of the role you have in mind for them. It's just like a sports team: a good goalkeeper won't necessarily be able to play centre-forward. So be aware of what team 'positions' you need to fill. At the same time, don't be frightened to change team personnel and team roles, especially if you think the team is becoming a little stale and unproductive.

3. **Focus on results**

   Be clear about what the purpose of the team is and what you want them to achieve. It could be a one-off task like setting up a new quiet study room, or an ongoing task such as ensuring teaching materials remain up to date. Time frames will also need to be clear and the following points addressed: how often the team should meet, how much time they will need to complete the project, and, perhaps most importantly, how they will record what they have done.

4. **Establish a team identity**

   Teams should always be clearly identified, along with their function and purpose, and known to all, even to those who do not have any involvement with what the team is doing. When teaching young learners, team identity is expressed through the use of coloured badges and branded banners. This may not be appropriate for staff working with adults, but identities can still be established in more subtle ways, such as through regular team meetings and by cross-reporting to other sectors.

5. **Discuss successful teams**

   Discuss teamwork and team-building in meetings. For example, one useful task is to get everyone to think about successful teams that they have been involved in in the past – as children, as a family, at school, as well as at work. Find out what made the team successful or unsuccessful. Encourage staff to reflect on how team successes from the past can be replicated and introduced in their present school.

6. Include team-building in professional development

There are a number of other team-building activities that can be used to create a focused working atmosphere; for example, joint lesson-planning, team teaching, peer observation, job swaps and cross-training for administrative staff. You can also try more creative activities, such as getting teams to design the perfect school using a limited supply of pens, paper and other materials in a limited time frame. The teams can then present their ideas in a poster or an actual model. Observing how the individual team members work together can tell you a lot about the skills and potential of your staff.

7. Regular team-bonding events

Team-bonding activities can be a regular feature on the staff social calendar. They don't need to be grand events such as corporate-style survival or paint-balling. A team-bonding activity can be something as simple and low-budget as a meal out, a sports day, a walk or an awayday. If someone different organises it, say, every term or semester, then there will be natural variety.

8. The 'buzz' team

Use small select teams to perform specific tasks. Each team can be seen as a kind of 'buzz team' or 'hit squad', with the team being disbanded as soon as the task is complete. The task can be something as mundane as tidying the teachers' room or putting together a proposal for a session at an ELT conference.

9. The fully random team

Select team members at random from across the full range of staff and stakeholders, including students and ancillary staff, to focus on a specific issue. The issue may relate to a topic area that is not specifically part of their job or interests. Topics that work well for random teams include: being more environmentally aware, improving punctuality, making better use of free time and living more healthily.

10. Celebrate team success

In sport, a successful team will win a trophy or some other prize, and their success will be described in the media. Schools can do something similar. A reward for a successful team project might simply be a mention in a meeting, an announcement at assembly (e.g. in summer schools), a voucher for learning materials or a day off.

Imagine that your entire school – students, teachers, administration, managers – has been abandoned on a desert island. For complicated geo-political reasons, there is no prospect of rescuing you for six months. You have a full supply of food and water and all the things you would expect on a big ship (apart from communication systems). The decision has been made that you will continue the work of the school as best you can. Thinking about the people in your school and knowing their various skills, decide what teams you need, what their roles and purposes will be, and who will be in each team.

10 reasons why meetings don't work

Meetings have always been the principal communication device that keeps organisations functioning and developing, from cave dwellers gathered round the fire to world leaders discussing international issues by video-link. For the ELT manager, meetings take various forms; for example, participants might all be in the same room or they might be using video chat software. Meetings also have a variety of purposes, such as communicating information about timetables, discussing student progress or inviting administrative staff to give their opinions on processes. Meetings can make the job of management easier but if not done well they can also have a negative influence and can lead to a static culture of apathy. Understanding the reasons why meetings sometimes do not work can help us to ensure that those in our school work efficiently and effectively.

1. They don't achieve anything

Language schools have lots of meetings: morning administration meetings, teachers' meetings, grading meetings and so on. Unfortunately, some are held simply 'because we always have a meeting at this time'. As a result, they can be unproductive, they can prevent development, they can stifle creativity, and they can inadvertently maintain the status quo. Ensure that there is a specific purpose for your meeting and identify clear intended outcomes, without dictating what those outcomes should be in advance. State the purpose in proactive terms, for example: 'To review issues arising in the previous week and to preview new student inductions, starting next week'. If there is no purpose, then don't have the meeting.

2. They go on too long and one or two people dominate

Some people love to talk at meetings; others are happy to be passive or may want to contribute but don't get the opportunity. It is important to establish some guidelines (which may be different for different types of meeting). There are several ways you can do this: you can start by making sure the purpose of the meeting is clear and that there is a time limit. Other rules might include appointing someone to keep an eye on the time and to keep the meeting moving, establishing protocols for turn-taking and turn-giving, and making sure the focus is on achieving outcomes.

3. The role of the person chairing the meeting is not clear

Ensure that all participants, including the chair themselves, know what the role of the chair is. Their priority can sometimes be just to get through the agenda as quickly as possible. Are they a listener, a facilitator, a referee or a dictator? The meeting needs to know. The chair should define their role and their way of working from the outset. The chair does not always have to be the boss. In fact, taking turns to chair meetings can make them more interesting and enjoyable.

4. Meetings always follow the same format

Meetings can become habit-bound, and will often take place in a room around a table; the room might even be called the 'meeting room'. As a first step, take down any 'meeting room' sign. Different types of meetings may require different locations, different formats, different furniture layouts, different times of day and different equipment. Think about how you want the furniture arranged to maximise the effectiveness of the meeting: a circle, a horseshoe, rows, desks/no desks, islands. For variety, introduce features such as a short presentation or video to set the scene.

5. The wrong people are sitting in the chairs

Make sure you choose the right attendees to make the meeting productive and interesting. It shouldn't always be the same people. To enhance the quality of the meeting and to build a team ethos, invite internal guests to bring a different perspective to the meeting: maybe a teacher at a management meeting, a student at a teachers' meeting.

6. Technology is not used effectively

Video-conferencing is an integral part of business communication. Make sure the application and online platform you choose are appropriate to the purpose of the meeting, and that the technology works and is set up in advance. Give pre-meeting guidance and training to attendees, and be aware of differing levels of digital competence. Establish communication protocols. Beware of information overload: organise content so that it is accessible and relevant, and, as always, focus on outcomes.

7. Agendas are long and tedious

It's important to have an agenda that is short, meaningful and circulated in advance with any relevant notes attached. Try to keep the number of points on the agenda down to five or six, and send it to participants at least 24 hours before the meeting. Make sure the purpose of the meeting is clear. At the end of the meeting, recap on what was discussed and agreed. Alternatively, try dispensing with the agenda altogether. Going 'agenda-free' once every four meetings, say, can be liberating, and can refresh subsequent agenda-based meetings.

8. There is no effective follow-up

You can have a very productive meeting, but if you don't follow up effectively it will count for very little. Circulate a summary of the outcomes with action points to all relevant people, including those who may not have been at the meeting. Allocate follow-up tasks to individuals, and give deadlines; for example, 'Jane to investigate new young learners coursebook for summer courses by 5 May'. Record the progress of the action plan in a spreadsheet with headings such as: Item, Action required, By who, By when, Progress, Complete. See page 166 of the Appendix for a template you can use to create an action plan.

9. **Meetings are boring**

   With the best will in the world, meetings can be uninteresting. One way of dealing with this is to consider alternative approaches to meetings. Varying the time and the location and rotating the chair have already been suggested. Another approach could be to have a standing meeting, perhaps with a table at the right height (but no chairs). Decisions tend to be taken more quickly when participants are standing. The meeting could even take place in a café or a garden, as opposed to an office. Alternatively, for small meetings with two or three participants, hold a walking meeting with points to discuss but no precise route. On your return to the office, summarise your final decisions.

10. **Positive outcomes are not made clear**

    Sometimes getting through the meeting seems to be an end in itself. Make sure that something positive emerges from every meeting. This can be done by asking every participant to identify a positive outcome, even if it seems insignificant. Some prompts might be useful; for example, ask participants to complete sentences such as: 'We talked about the difficult issue concerning…', 'We came up with a good idea for…', 'We maintained a positive approach to…' and 'I realised that…'.

    Think of three meetings you have attended or run in recent months. Include at least one successful and one unsuccessful meeting. Complete the template on page 167 of the Appendix and then establish ten general rules of your own for meetings.

10 things you can do with a decision

We all have to make decisions in our working and personal life. Decision-making is an indispensable and continuous part of the manager's role, and is arguably the most important function. Staff and students will look to managers for decisions, and will judge the manager according to the effectiveness and impact of the decisions taken.

1. **Be decisive**

    Don't prevaricate: leadership is about decision-making. But don't rush it either. Knee-jerk decisions are rarely the best ones, so give yourself some time to consider the nature and the context of the decision you have to make. Make bulleted lists of pros and cons on the back of an envelope or call an emergency meeting of staff whose input you would benefit from.

2. **Consult others**

    Talk to a variety of people to help you make your decision. Don't just consult your obvious supporters, but include your critics (or at least imagine what their views will be, if the decision is likely to be controversial). Give genuine consideration to alternatives, even if you do not think they would work. Make sure that the consultation phase is recorded, particularly if it relates to a big decision.

3. **Assess before you announce**

    Check you've got the details right. Before you announce the decision, stop for a moment. Sleep on it if possible. Take time to assess again whether it is a good decision and what the consequences will be for everyone involved, including yourself. Think about the impact outside the school on other stakeholders, agents, clients and competitors. For each route that you decide not to take, force yourself to complete the sentence: 'This won't work because…'

4. **Monitor it**

    Decisions come in all sizes, and they all need monitoring, even if it's just a question of whether to move a student to another class or whether to give a teacher more hours. If it is a big decision, such as introducing a digital-based learning curriculum and virtual learning environment (VLE), then you need to create an action plan (see page 166 for a template) to implement the consequences and monitor the progress of the decision.

5. **Develop it**

    Making a decision is sometimes only the start of a process. You may need not only to monitor the decision, but also to modify it. As you implement the decision, think of ways you can make it better and stronger. Bring other people in to take the development to a further stage; for example, to develop further applications for the VLE in terms of post-course study and associated marketing opportunities.

6. **Tell someone about it**

    To test a decision with a degree of objectivity, tell a friend or a family member rather than the people who have been involved in or affected by the decision. They will be able to provide an outsider's view. With the benefit of an external perspective, you might be able to refine the decision.

7. Ditch it

If your decision turns out to have been the wrong one, be prepared to accept the fact. Admitting you made a wrong decision is a sign of flexibility and is likely to make you a better manager and win you respect – but not if it happens too frequently! Remember, too, that sometimes it might not be the decision that was bad, but the implementation of it.

8. Repair any damage done

If your decision turns out to have been the wrong one, just dropping it will not be enough. As a manager you can't just shrug your shoulders and move on. Instead, you will have to work to retrieve the successful parts of the decision and to remedy any problems caused.

9. Evaluate and learn from it

As well as evaluating the success or otherwise of the decision itself, evaluate your own performance. What could you have done better? Did you consult, share, assess, monitor and develop the decision effectively? Are you a better manager as a result? Self-assessment is an important way to improve your professional skills in general.

10. Prioritise your decisions

Managers rarely have the luxury of being able to work on a single issue. In a typical working day you may have many decisions to make. At the start of the day – and also as the day progresses – rate the importance and urgency of each decision. To do this, you can use this simple matrix. Make a list of things you have to do during your working day and then categorise them using this table.

	Urgent	Not urgent
Important		
Not important		

> *"School managers make on the spot decisions every day, but the big decisions need to be thought through carefully and agreement reached with staff whenever possible. Decisions made without consultation are likely to make implementation much more difficult."*

Roger Gower, School inspector and ex-school principal

10 reasons why change may fail

Change is an inevitable fact of life for all members of any organisation, perhaps especially so for those language schools which run short term courses with a high turnover of students (and teachers). All schools will be affected by changing approaches to learning, not to mention economic and social changes. Learning how to manage change (and to manage your staff and students through change), whether it is initiated by you or imposed on you, is one of the key skills of the effective strategic manager and their team. One key point to remember is that you do not need to be alone in this.

1. Failure to take control of change

If you embrace change and take control of it, you will have an effective operational tool and a positive developmental opportunity, even if it involves difficult decisions. First, you need to identify the change factors (i.e. what exactly is changing) and who and what they impact on. Secondly, give your change project a clear identity (e.g. 'Introducing a new range of course options to attract students on low budgets'). Then produce an implementation plan that describes the details and stages needed to complete your project.

2. Failure to understand how difficult the task is

While some people embrace change, many others are afraid of it. Even the smallest adjustment to their role and routine, let alone the terms and conditions of their employment, can take them out of their comfort zone and set alarm bells ringing. Managers must never underestimate or dismiss this fear. Start by identifying everyone who will be affected by the proposed change, however small their involvement might be. Talk to those people, discuss and listen to their concerns, and explain the reasons why the change is taking place. As the implementation plan proceeds, keep an open door for staff or stakeholders to express their concerns.

3. Failure to provide sufficient resources

Change is resource-hungry, so you need to be prepared to spend money and time on it. Regularly assess the progress of your implementation plan, and allocate resources as required. Resources might include research, surveys, focus groups, trialling, incentives, emergency facilities, or even a party. With planned change (i.e. proactive change initiated by you), resource needs should be more predictable and easier to control. But with unplanned change (i.e. reactive external change not initiated by you), resource needs could be less predictable and you will need to have contingency and emergency resources in place.

4. Failure to create a strong guiding coalition

Implementing change by yourself can be lonely, inefficient and counter-productive. Always take a team approach, but think very carefully about who the team members should be. The team will be a guiding coalition. Their role is to guide everyone through the period of change, so they need to be representative of all the people affected. As a coalition, they will not share the same views, but they should understand and share the ultimate purpose of the change project. The guiding coalition should meet and consult regularly, and should engage with all departments within your school. Include the doubters and the cynics: remember that resistance is not always an attempt to block, but is often a cry for help and inclusion, and can be based on experience of previous change.

5. Failure to appreciate the power of a vision

A vision can be a powerful thing and your change project can be seen as part of your journey to achieving that vision, rather than an annoying obstacle to be overcome. Imagine gazing up at the sun-drenched summit of a mountain: there are rock faces and crevasses to conquer in order to reach the summit, and there will be long periods when the summit disappears, so it is important to keep the vision in mind and to communicate that vision to the stakeholders. Remind people what you are trying to achieve and the purpose of all the effort involved in implementing change. It can be something as simple as displaying a picture of the mountain summit.

6. Failure to overcome obstacles that block the vision

Obstacles that block the vision may appear insurmountable and it may feel easier just to abandon the change project, or to compromise on a simpler outcome. But overcoming an obstacle can be an empowering experience and will often make it easier to face further obstacles. There are various tactics you can use: (1) predict what the obstacles might be (e.g. teacher resistance, budgetary constraints), (2) reflect on how to deal with them, and (3) appoint a member of your guiding coalition to have special responsibility for responding to any challenges that arise.

7. Failure to recognise short-term wins

Change is a process; it will rarely be achieved overnight. It is important to acknowledge and celebrate each successful stage. Use a simple diagram of the proposed journey and the numbered stages you need to go through, maybe in the form of a mountain. But don't fixate on the soaring peak of the mountain in the distance; instead, focus on each stage as your prime target: the journey to the base camp, then onto camp 2, camp 3 and so on until the final ascent and the raising of the flag. Keep a diary or video log and use pictures and comments from the members of the team as they follow their journey.

8. Failure to secure changes in the culture of the organisation

Fundamental strategic change, such as moving your school to a new location in a different city, the introduction of a completely new curriculum, or the restructuring of employment contracts, may involve the need to change the culture and ethos of your organisation, and require people to think and behave in a different way. Maintaining a positive approach to new behavioural requirements is essential. Identify the behaviours required (such as how to deal with setbacks and how to encourage the doubters) and provide training and support accordingly. You must also be prepared to lose those people who will not or cannot buy into the new culture.

9. **Failure to see it through to the end**

   Sometimes it all seems too much and we give up, or leave a project dangling half-finished. For example, you introduce a new and exciting course, but do not manage to sell it to your agents or potential students. Don't give up immediately, but take some time out: think about where you are, consult and discuss with your guiding coalition, consider possible alternatives and their consequences. Giving up is often not an easy option: it can be seen as a wasteful expense or you may lose face. Also be careful not to declare victory too soon. When you are nearing the fulfilment of your change project and you have achieved what you wanted, there can be a tendency to forget the loose ends that need tying up. The finalising of these details is, however, important in securing the success of your project. Old habits can often creep back in, so monitoring the continuing implementation of change will be essential.

10. **Failure to realise that you need to do it all again tomorrow**

    Do not rest on your laurels. There will be other challenges and changes to manage, and although they may be very different, you can still learn from the experience of previous projects. Learn not only to expect change, but also to love it!

    Using the lessons learnt in this unit, try some scenario planning for yourself. Look at the scenarios below and choose one that relates to a change you are planning on implementing. Decide which is affected and produce an implementation plan that avoids the pitfalls mentioned in the previous tips.

    A. Closing or downsizing a city-centre branch and opening a new branch outside the city.

    B. Investing in cutting-edge digital technology.

    C. Re-issuing new contracts to all staff with less generous rates of pay, holiday entitlement, job security, etc.

> "Leading change is not for perfectionists, because the perfectionist may never get it off the ground. You need people who will take educated risks – I don't mean the impetuous but people who think it through and then just go for it. Change is for those with a vision, who can achieve something that is significantly new (albeit imperfect) and then make it consistently better by experience."
>
> **Mark Lindsay, Managing Director, St Giles International**

10 tips for making HR human

Some schools may be big enough to have a human resources (HR) department; others may have access to an HR consultant who can advise on HR issues. For other organisations, human resources matters are dealt with by the school managers. Human resources can often be associated with unpleasant elements of the workplace such as disciplinaries, performance management and redundancies; however, it covers much more than that. Recruitment and contracts, changes in employment law and matters of compliance, keeping mandatory policy and procedure up to date and ensuring everyone is informed all come under the umbrella of HR. It is important to remember that when dealing with any HR-related matters, procedures and policy should be followed. It is also crucial to apply fairness, transparency and an awareness that we are dealing with people. What follows are 10 tips on how we can do this within our roles.

1. Remain objective

It is easy for things to get personal when you're dealing with staff issues, even if it is a mild disciplinary warning with a teacher. A good way of staying objective is to prepare in advance what you want to say and to establish what the ideal outcome of an HR meeting with a staff member would be. Rehearse how you are going to conduct the meeting and be careful not to over-repeat your message – a common mistake people make when giving bad news or dealing with a tricky situation. However, don't script a meeting either, as that would leave no space for flexibility.

2. Show fairness to all staff

Have clear policies and procedures in place, which are accessible and known by all teaching and administrative staff (see Unit 17 on policy statements and handbooks). It is important to implement these fairly and consistently across the board. Do not show favouritism, but do show understanding and empathy when dealing with difficult situations such as an argument between two teachers or a cultural issue between teacher and student. In order to be fair, gather all the facts and details when implementing any HR policy. This may involve interviewing people and getting written statements from all involved before deciding on the way forward. Document everything: you never know when you might need to refer to it. Always put yourself in the other person's shoes and do not make it personal.

3. Don't act on impulse

If you are dealing with a challenging situation such as a disciplinary meeting, do not act impulsively. Give any situation space and time so that emotions being brought to the meeting are minimised. This is easier said than done as it is also important to act in a timely fashion, especially if the situation is serious or puts somebody at risk. If something is not dealt with soon after an incident, it leaves everyone wondering about the consequences. Refer to the written procedure in place to help guide you and structure what action to take. An example of a challenging situation might be if one member of staff offended another and an argument ensued. Such arguments can take place in the teachers' room or another public place in the school. Think about how you would deal with this and what timeline you would put in place. If a teacher is involved, you need to take into consideration the fact that they should not be subjected to a stressful disciplinary situation just before going into class.

4. Keep a record

Whenever you deal with a staff issue or any area of HR, keep an accurate record of the situation, of action taken and proposed further action. When dealing with a small issue, this can be useful to build a picture of behaviour. Something which seems small in isolation can evolve into a pattern of behaviour. For example, a teacher's sick record, once recorded and monitored, may show a pattern of sick days at certain times of the week or month. Keeping a record allows you to notice this, bring it to the person's attention and discuss whether there is any serious underlying problem. Another reason to record any incident or meeting is that a matter which feels small can develop into something more serious before you know it. Therefore, it is important to have all details documented from the start. Everything you write about an employee and meetings which have taken place may also be shared with the staff member in the future (for example, if a matter escalates), so keep your notes factual and to the point. It is best practice to provide a member of staff with a written summary of any meeting you have had so that both sides are clear about what has been discussed and agreed. This might constitute a capability plan for underperformance in the classroom.

5. Understanding can't versus won't

When dealing with staff underperformance, it is crucial to know the difference between a capability procedure and a disciplinary. 'Capability' relates to a situation in which a staff member can't perform to any better a standard, for example, in the case of a teacher struggling with an ESP class and receiving constant negative feedback. This may be because they do not have the tools and resources to do so or because extra training, support and experience are needed. Disciplinary action is taken when a staff member *won't* perform to standard, possibly due to dissatisfaction, lack of interest or being stuck in a rut. It is important to understand the cause of any underperformance situation in order to know which course of action to take. When underperformance is due to capability, the manager can work with the individual to put a plan of support (a 'capability plan' or 'performance improvement plan') in place. (See page 168 for an example of a performance improvement plan (PIP) for an underperforming teacher.) When an employee seems to have made a choice not to perform to the expected standard, it is equally important to establish whether there are underlying reasons which can be addressed. For example, if the person in question is just bored, perhaps because they have been with the organisation doing the same job for a long time, a new challenge may help.

6. Consider the good of the school

Think of the good of your students and organisation in any HR decision you make, from offering a permanent teaching position to terminating a contract, to anything in the middle. It can be tempting (and easier) to bend the rules to make exceptions for a staff member. However, doing this can create bigger problems in the long run: it can be detrimental to the team, as well as to their respect for and belief in the school ethos and policies. At the same time, do keep the 'human' in HR: try to see things through the staff member's eyes when conducting a meeting or dealing with HR matters. People may not always like what they hear in a meeting with their manager but everyone appreciates fairness, honesty and transparency.

7. Respect confidentiality

Staff may feel they have a right to know the details when there is an issue with a colleague, such as a grievance or disciplinary action for some breach of policy. This is common in a teaching team as they work as a close group. However, it is crucial that only the people directly involved should have access to the details of the situation. You must treat any matter with confidentiality, even though there may be a temptation to share your thoughts with staff in order to let them know a matter is being appropriately dealt with. Instead, ask your staff to trust that you are dealing with any issue in an appropriate way, and request that they respect the privacy of the colleague in question. With this in mind, documentation of events should be factual, dated and not accessible by others. Always be prepared to show any documentation if a case is taken to a higher level such as a tribunal.

8. Defuse matters, don't escalate them

When a day-to-day staff dispute arises, it is advisable to start with a gentle informal approach rather than a heavy-handed one. For example: two teachers have an argument over a lack of liaising about a class; it becomes public and voices are raised. Don't jump straight into a formal, documented meeting; instead, arrange a time to sit down and conduct a more informal mediation meeting with the aim of encouraging the teachers to acknowledge their inappropriate behaviour, to apologise to each other, and to show more respect in the future.

9. Making changes to terms and conditions

This is one of the more difficult areas that managers need to deal with. As time goes on in the life of a school, terms and conditions can become outdated and no longer beneficial to the running of the business. One example of this might involve teaching and non-teaching hours: in the past, staff may have been employed to work between 9am and 5pm, but that may not allow the school to meet the demands of students for courses at other times. Plan your approach to introducing any change very carefully. Involve a staff spokesperson to represent the rest of the team if you have a big teaching staff. You will then enter a period of consultation, outlining clearly the proposed change and the reason for it. If possible, offer something in exchange. You should have a clear timeline for staff to express their concerns and to offer alternatives before they are then asked to sign to say that they accept the change. This sounds straightforward, but be prepared for a period of negotiation during which you will need to be flexible in order for the process to go smoothly.

10. Dealing with legal action and tribunals

Sometimes no matter how much we try to smooth things over, a situation can escalate and lead to legal action being taken, either by an individual, the school, a customer (student/agent/parent) or a group of employees. This is stressful and upsetting for all involved. It is important to remain objective and to tackle the issue rather than make it personal. Seek legal advice, document everything, and don't forget to look after your own well-being throughout. Ensure that you have support from your line manager and from the organisation.

10 steps to successful recruitment

Recruitment is a key area in the successful running of any language school. Getting it right from the start allows the staff to believe in the vision and mission of your school. New staff will provide further opportunities for the school to develop, but the wrong person can completely change the dynamics of your team and disrupt aspects of your school. It is therefore important that you are clear about who you want for the post, and that the role is clearly defined. This applies to any role, whether academic or administrative.

1. Define the role and the person

Ensure that you have a crystal-clear idea of the position that is vacant and the person you want. Consider the ethos and vision of the school and the team, and analyse where you have skills gaps. In order to become familiar with this process, it is advisable to revisit (and rewrite if necessary) the job description and person specification each time you recruit, even if it is for the same position. Where possible, involve more than one person in this update. Then decide how open you will be to compromise (and in what areas) if your number-one candidate does not tick every box.

2. Advertising

Use the person specification and job description to construct your advertisement. Remember to tap into social media and your professional networks when advertising. This is possibly the first contact your new member of staff will have with your organisation, so it is important to get your message and expectations across clearly from this early stage. Outline the benefits of working with your organisation: the ELT job market is becoming more and more competitive, so show off what the new recruit will gain from working with your school, for example, developmental opportunities, travel and career path.

3. Shortlisting

Choose your recruitment team at the start of the process. Whether you are advertising for a teacher or a member of your administrative team, it is best practice to have two people shortlisting applications independently, working from agreed criteria. The criteria should be consistent with and dictated by the job description, job advert and person specification. A joined-up and consistent process should ensure you get the right people on the shortlist.

4. The interview(s)

Decide beforehand on a clear structure. Will you have one or two rounds of interviewing? How will the recruitment team feed back to each other following interviews? What does the decision-making process involve? Will you include a task? It is advisable to involve as many key staff members as possible. For example, you could ask a non-interviewing staff member to provide a tour of the school. This is a time when an applicant may relax and open up, so although short, it might be a perfect opportunity to get an honest insight into the candidate's thoughts and behaviour.

5. The questions

Decide beforehand on a set of questions (see page 169 of the Appendix for a list of suggested questions). Include questions that allow the candidate to draw on their experience. Ask open-ended questions and provide scenarios. If you are not getting a full enough answer, it is important to go into a topic more deeply. Don't ask trick questions: you want to get the best from the person and make them feel at ease. Try to avoid leading questions, too. Although you have a template of questions, don't be afraid to deviate, especially when addressing experience from the CV or application form. It is important to probe and to allow candidates to elaborate on responses. When interviewing for teaching roles, ask for real and recent examples of teaching practice. Always ensure that your questions are tailored to your school and the job in question. Crucially, you should include some 'safer recruitment' questions. Examples of these might be:

- What would you consider inappropriate behaviour between a student and teacher?
- Have you ever noticed behaviour in a staff member that concerned you? If so, what did you do?
- How would you ensure your classroom or school was a safe environment for students to study in?

6. The interview task

A task can be a useful way of getting an insight into a candidate's working style and capabilities. Keep the task consistent and relevant to the role. For example, when interviewing for a teaching role, ask candidates to draw up a brief lesson plan from materials provided to present the present perfect to a group of intermediate adult students. Let the candidate know in advance that there will be a task and how long this will take. Decide in advance how much weighting will be given to successful task performance. Tasks could include: giving a short presentation, solving a problem or, more specifically for non-teaching positions, completing a number of smaller tasks to test how candidates deal in quick succession with a number of emails, requests and issues that 'land on their desk'.

7. Timeline

Recruitment is a time-consuming process, so it is important to draw up a timeline in advance. This should be communicated to all staff involved to ensure they can factor it into their working week. It is also a good idea to have a timeline for the period from the start of the recruitment process to the actual appointment. It is advisable to appoint fairly quickly after the decision has been made in order to avoid losing a strong candidate. On the other hand, there will be occasions when it is necessary to wait or to re-advertise the post to ensure you get someone you really want.

8. **Decision making**

    Establish your criteria for selection, weighing up all factors carefully in a measured and fair way. Include the opinions of everyone who was part of the process. Criteria should be based on what was advertised, along with the skills and experience stated in the job description and person specification. Ensure that you have evidence to back up your decision to avoid focusing too much on one particular aspect of a candidate that you liked. However, do listen to your gut feeling too, as this is often based on some underlying factor. Don't be afraid to re-advertise if you don't find the right person.

9. **Offering the position**

    Offer the position in writing, outlining the start date, the salary and the conditions. Describe the induction procedure briefly to provide assurance that there will be sufficient on-the-job training. Give a deadline for acceptance and, if possible, don't reject your shortlist until you have an acceptance. Make sure all qualifications are checked and authenticated. State that the position is dependent on references, a police check, or any other requirements of the job. Be sure to arrange for the contract to be issued soon after acceptance.

10. **Fast-track teacher recruitment**

    For temporary or summer teacher recruitment, you may not have the luxury of such a full procedure as the one described above. Think of ways of reducing the time and stages involved in the nine previous steps of recruitment. What points can you definitely not drop from your process? For example, you might be able to make a decision after only one interview rather than two, and that interview could take place over Skype, if necessary.

> *"Recruitment is about much more than qualifications and experience – culture fit is key. You can train and support new staff but if their work values do not fit those of your organisation, you will have problems."*
>
> **Gillian Davidson, Group Academic Director, EC English**

10 ways of achieving staff loyalty

As we saw in Unit 15, getting recruitment right is a lengthy but crucial process. It is therefore important that new staff members feel part of the organisation as soon as possible and have a desire to invest their time, energy and hard work in the school. Longevity of service is positive, as long as long-term members of staff feel valued and are given the opportunity to develop and contribute to the organisation. The benefits of good retention of staff are many: an opportunity to develop good new recruits, long-term knowledge of the workings of the school, continuity and consistency, relationship building with clients, time and cost saving in repeat recruitment and training, to name a few. What follows are some ideas to help make retention successful.

1. **Wow them**

    From the minute a new member of staff has contact with your school, they will start to make judgements about it. It is important to make them feel from day one that they have made the right decision. This will go a long way to ensuring their investment in the school ethos. Consider the little details that will make them feel valued and special on day one, week one and month one. They do not need to be attended to at great expense – they can be small things like sending a welcome email, sending an email again at the end of their day to say you are glad they are part of team, ensuring all staff members know the name and role of the new person, and ensuring their work space is theirs and not left over from the last person. If you want to spend some money, arrange welcome drinks or provide a cake at coffee break. Remember not to stop 'wowing' staff and making them feel appreciated after the first month.

2. **Induction or 'onboarding'**

    Whatever the role and whatever the length of contract, it is important to have a full and ongoing induction plan in place to help the new person settle in and perform well from day one. This will also help other staff members and clients, so investing the time in a structured induction is worth the effort. The term 'onboarding' refers to the same concept – the process of integrating a new employee into an organisation. The first day can be overwhelming, so cover only the most important things initially. Then spread the induction over the space of several weeks, checking that all is going well by way of post-induction meetings. Don't forget that even after six months your new employee will still be new to some aspects of the role. It could be argued that a full induction lasts 12 months, the full life cycle of a school and all the roles within it.

3. **Mentors**

    Arrange for new staff members to have a mentor. Clearly define the mentor's role and ensure that the existing staff member is happy to take this role on. A mentor is often a colleague who can provide support and answer the little questions a new staff member may feel too shy to ask their line manager. A successful mentoring system can establish strong friendships or at the least good professional respect between colleagues. When choosing a mentor, consider the personality compatibility of the pairing.

4. Goal-setting meetings

Establish a pattern of regular, individual support meetings with staff, especially for the first few months of their term. This is an opportunity to check how they are settling in, how they are getting to grips with their role, to establish goals and communicate expectations. It is also, very importantly, a place to provide meaningful positive feedback. When this system is in place it will establish a feeling of being valued. Get this right from the start and you should have staff loyalty in return. If your organisation is big or spread out, or your team members work at various times, try to implement these meetings virtually if a face-to-face option is not possible.

5. Complacency

As a manager, it is easy to lose sight of the needs of your longer-term members of staff. Do not become complacent and take these people for granted just because they seem settled or because everything is going well. Providing support and individualised praise and recognition is not time-consuming, so distribute it evenly and generously. Take the time to ask how team members are doing and take an interest in their responses. This can provide an opportunity for a long-term member of staff to share concerns they have about their place in the organisation rather than just resigning without warning.

6. Workload

It is important to capitalise on people's strengths. These will become apparent as a person grows into a role. The role should grow and change with the person you have in place, and as a result the job description evolves. With this in mind, be aware of how much work an individual is taking on and how many additional tasks are being added to a person's role. Fairly new members of staff tend to be eager to please, so be careful not to pile work on them because they don't say no. They may end up burning out or leaving the school.

7. Training and development

A key to staff retention, and particularly the retention of happy staff, is to ensure they are motivated and stimulated by their work, and that they feel their development is adding to the development of the school. In a language school, we often associate professional development with the teaching staff. However, everyone benefits from development in their roles, so ensure that professional development opportunities are provided in all departments and to all members of staff. Ensure that clear, agreed developmental goals are in place and provide the means to make them achievable. Training does not need to be all about diplomas and MAs, but can be as straightforward as training the staff in how to promote the new courses the school has introduced. Cross-departmental training and sharing of experiences contributes to understanding the value of others, which in turn creates a more harmonious team and therefore a good working environment. See Units 41 and 42 for further tips on training and development.

8. Review your Ts and Cs

In most countries English language teaching exists in a saturated market. Employees will look around, and if your competitors are offering better working conditions than you they may leave. Do a regular salary review to ensure you remain competitive. What other perks or benefits can you provide? Think of holiday allowance, free tea and coffee, training provision, opportunities for promotion and career advancement. Add these into your staff handbook or induction document so that staff know that the school values and invests in them. Pay is not always the main motivator for staying in a job but the little extras show the staff that they are valued, and they go a long way towards helping retain staff.

9. Trust and communication

Your team is your biggest asset. Listen to them, show an interest, ask for their opinions and suggestions, get to know 'the whole person' and take their concerns seriously. Building a culture of trust is complex and fluid, but it is appreciated by staff and will lead to effective retention and investment from your team. One way of doing this is to organise out-of-school get-togethers to build a sense of community. This could be something as simple as going for a walk together, cooking lunch as a team or doing a training workshop with an underlying goal of bringing people together.

10. Find out about your staff

It is useful to look at your staff profile from time to time. Keen new members of staff can become long-term staff members, and this can be positive or negative for the team dynamic, depending on their reasons for staying and the extent to which they feel valued. It's useful to carry out mini-interviews or do a survey with your staff to get an overall picture of the team on a regular basis. Find out why your staff stay, what they appreciate, and what they would like more or less of in the workplace. Use the results to identify ways of improving staff conditions, understanding how you are perceived, and hopefully as a result encouraging people to stay with you for the right reasons. See page 171 of the Appendix for an example of a staff satisfaction survey form. Think how you could modify it to suit your team.

> *"We should be looking for every opportunity to promote the engagement and performance of employees through building and maintaining relationships; creating and encouraging a culture of collaboration; promoting learning; recognising and rewarding achievements; and solving individual problems which may positively impact on many. In a nutshell, HR should be about making everyone's working lives simpler, productive, better and happier."*
>
> **Tommy King, Beststart Human Resources – HR Consultancy, UK**

10 tips for writing policy statements and the staff handbook

Having a staff handbook and a bank of policy statements provides transparency and guidance for all staff on the way the organisation operates. The policies will be a combination of legislative procedures, such as information on equal opportunities, parental leave, etc., and policies set by the school, such as those surrounding annual leave and the procedure for covering absent teachers. In order for a staff handbook or compilation of school policies to be relevant and useful it should be reviewed annually and shared with all staff. The handbook may also provide clear guidance on how general tasks should be carried out in the school. In larger organisations with many different departments and roles, it is also beneficial to have departmental or role manuals to describe the various jobs and tasks in detail. Keep this manual role- or department-specific as the extra pages would make an all-staff handbook cumbersome, with much of the content being irrelevant to the majority of readers.

1. The contents
Do not reinvent the wheel when constructing your staff handbook. Many schools have some form of staff handbook or document of school guidelines so talk to friends, colleagues or teaching associations to ask if they are willing to share at least a list of contents. Also, seek input and advice from the HR department (if there is one). You can also look to other industries to see what they have in terms of staff guidelines and policies. See page 172 of the Appendix for a list of suggested policies.

2. Staff involvement
Involve key members of staff when establishing what the school policies are. For example, if you have a welfare officer, they should lead on writing a safeguarding policy. Involving the relevant members of staff ensures that the policies and procedures documents reflect what is actually happening in the school. It also highlights, and allows you to iron out, any less acceptable practices and procedures. Finally, it creates staff buy-in and a belief in the handbook.

3. Style
Write each policy with the reader in mind. Keep it clear, detailed, logical and to the point. Avoid jargon and management-speak. Each policy should be easily identifiable, and readers should be able to refer to them in isolation. If it is easy to read and relevant to the reader, rather than a heavy, dense document that is rarely referred to, it will be a more useful document for all staff.

4. Preparation
Writing a staff handbook is not a quick job for one person only. Dedicate the time it warrants to putting it together. Set realistic time limits and, where possible, working groups, who will review the policies and procedures included in the handbook. The person who writes should not be the person who proofreads, so involve several people in the checking process. At the end of the process, ask yourself if the document gives a full and fair picture of the workings of the school.

5. Formalities

All school policies should be reviewed, dated and initialled annually. This will help to keep the policy documents current. Schedule this as an annual task. Policies should be signed off by the person responsible for implementing them, usually the school principal or director. The handbook can then be circulated to all staff, who will, where possible, sign a confirmation slip to confirm that they have read it. This can be done electronically; the point is that the act of signing as read puts the emphasis on staff to take responsibility for knowing the school policies, procedures and ethos. This will also help in any cases where there are disputes of policy, procedure or working practices.

6. New staff members

Ensure that new members of staff read and sign the handbook as part of their induction procedure. It is helpful to provide a quick 'need to know' cover page as well as a contents list as, by its nature, a staff handbook is a long document. The 'need to know' page for new staff members might include page references to safeguarding documents, health and safety procedures and any internal policies and procedures that will help them do their jobs with ease in the first few days and weeks. For a teacher, this could include a 'social media and internet in the classroom' policy, the 'day one' procedure for students, or the school's policy on dealing with absent students.

7. Introducing changes

Each policy should reflect what happens in school as best practice. It is important to provide an opportunity for staff to contribute to, and feed back on, any policies and changes that are made annually. This will create less of a top-down feel to the handbook and will also make it more likely that policies will be adhered to. Make sure you are transparent about any changes and updates. For example, at a teachers' meeting, you could present a one-page summary with page references to changes that have been made. Include explanations for the changes. Some changes may be required in order to move with the times; some may be a result of legislation, and some might relate to the way the school is evolving. Whatever you do, don't introduce a change to your school in a hidden way through the handbook just because you think there may be resistance to it.

8. Underestimating the result of a change

Plan carefully and in detail how to communicate changes in policy to teachers and staff in order for the change to be effective. Never take the acceptance of any change, no matter how small, for granted. Small changes that are not well communicated can lead to enormous staff dissatisfaction. Once the change has been communicated, put measures in place to ensure that it is being implemented. This relies on 'buy-in' from the managers who oversee any changes and structured monitoring from the start. Any change requires new habit-forming in order to be successful.

9. **The final check**

   Task at least one person who has an excellent eye for detail to proofread the document. They should not only look for typos but also check that any new policies or changes to existing ones are described consistently throughout the document. Finally, they should keep an eye out for any name changes that have been missed in updated sections. (Note, though, that it is usually advisable to avoid using people's names – use job titles instead.)

10. **Practicalities**

    Avoid keeping duplicate electronic documents in various places on the school system, and actively discourage all staff from doing the same. Save one master copy for staff reference (and deter people from printing it). Duplicate versions saved in departmental or personal files will lead to confusion as changes occur, with people following and referring to different and out-of-date policies and procedures on how to do things within the school.

> *"Having a clear, simple and commonly-understood staff handbook and policies will save any organisation leader a lot of time and stress, so it is well worth the effort to ensure they are done well. When writing or reviewing the staff handbook, it is always best practice to consult staff and be seen to take their views into account so that everyone feels involved and invested in the ownership of the document. Similarly, with policies, input from key stakeholders helps to ensure that your policies are relevant and followed properly. New staff induction procedures should always include the reading and understanding of these important documents."*
>
> **Violet McLaren, Ex-Headteacher at a UK primary school**

10 principles of efficient student administration

Robust student administration systems run through all departments and hold any school together. Without administrative systems, staff cannot do their jobs effectively: teachers cannot prepare for classes if they do not know how many students they have and what their levels are; schools cannot monitor whether they are making enough money to pay salaries; and students do not receive the customer care they expect. School administration systems often evolve and are adapted as time goes by, and as the school grows and changes. It is important to pay attention to whether the current systems are fit for purpose or whether there is room for improvement. Here are 10 points to keep in mind regarding student administration.

1. Remember the person

Every administrative action in a school has an impact on a person, be it a student, a staff member or another stakeholder. It is therefore important to remember that administration tasks are not 'just' administration tasks. For example, when moving a student to a different class, ask yourself why you are making this move, whether the student is aware of and happy about it, whether the student knows the room number and name of the teacher, and whether both class teachers are aware and understand the reasons for it. Ensure you provide accurate information when needed.

2. Remind others of the person

Work towards the principle that people are at the heart of everything you do administratively. Ensure that this idea is conveyed to others, especially teachers. Teachers often feel bogged down by administration tasks imposed on them from management. Make sure they know the thinking behind the tasks and understand how students might be affected, depending on whether they carry them out or not. In this way, a teacher is more likely to have faith in the system and is less likely to see the procedure as a 'tick-box exercise'. For example, if the teacher designs a clear course outline in student-friendly language and makes it accessible to the student in advance, the student will have faith in the fact that the teacher has planned the course with their learning needs in mind. If the teacher forgets to do the course outline, students might get the impression that the teacher is not prepared or has no interest in them, leading to frustration and complaints being made to the academic manager.

3. Monitor the effectiveness of your student systems

Make sure you have tried-and-tested systems in place. There should be clear instructions on how to carry out each administrative task so that the effectiveness of a task is not reliant on the knowledge held in one staff member's head. Do a systems review with those who use them and consider suggestions for improvements. Such a review is also a good opportunity for some cross-departmental training and feedback. It can provide a great opportunity to share best practice if you work in a large organisation, such as a secondary school or university. Finally, do not make knee-jerk changes out of frustration; instead, think things through logically.

4. **Transparency and feedback**

   It is mostly teachers who are at the receiving end of growing numbers of student administration tasks, so ensure that you have them on board. Think about how to do this and establish how you will introduce any changes or new systems. In addition, ensure details of classroom administration are clearly outlined in any induction documentation for new staff. Ask for and listen to feedback from teachers and their concerns. Teachers often have good ideas for modifying a system to help themselves and their students. You may even find some systems are now redundant and are just being done out of habit.

5. **Make changes**

   Be prepared to change a system if it is no longer doing what it should. Do not stick to the 'this is how we have always done it' mantra and do not be afraid to make a big change, as long as you have carefully considered the consequences beforehand. It is common to add bits on to an original system, but doing this can often lead to its becoming more complicated than necessary. For example, as the volume of safeguarding documentation for young students increases, it may be that your registration and documentation procedures are no longer robust enough. Do not be put off changing a system simply because doing so would be complicated or expensive. Rather than repeatedly adding to a database designed 20+ years ago, think how you might be able to start again with a new and simpler system for today's students. Once again, it is important to put the person at the forefront of the system when considering whether a system still works.

6. **Focus**

   Some student administrative tasks (such as setting up classes or allocating students and teachers appropriately to the timetable) can be complex and lengthy. Allow yourself set times, without interruption, at times of the day and week when you know you concentrate best. Let others know that you are not available for this block of time and, if necessary, remove yourself from your usual office in order to work through a task somewhere where you will not be disturbed.

7. **Be systematic**

   Go through each task systematically, ticking off when you have completed each part of it. For example, if one of your big regular tasks is preparing the teacher timetable for the following week or the following term, go through each change logically and without distractions. Use spreadsheets or apps to help you complete your to-do list in a systematic and clear way. Make these accessible to your colleagues so that they can understand your schedule and progress with tasks.

8. Dealing with problems

There will be administration problems from time to time, whether these are caused by human error, lack of communication or other outside factors such as a classroom no longer being available. Don't panic! There is always a solution, so stay calm and give yourself time to think creatively about what that solution could be. For example, if a room is no longer available, consider the options: are there other spaces in the school that could be used? Could you arrange a class excursion to get the students out of the building at that time? If you are in a secondary school or university, can you liaise with another department to find extra space? Or is it worth hiring extra space? Share your problem with other managers or staff members who are familiar with the student system. Search for solutions rather than apportioning blame. The important thing here is communication; communicate to those involved what has happened, apologise if necessary, and explain what you propose to do.

9. Be flexible with your routine

You may have a systematic routine for carrying out student administrative tasks. While doing this constitutes good planning, you should not let it rule your week. Know the latest deadline for each task, how long you need to complete it and the likely impact of any delays. For example, you may usually prepare the teaching timetable for the following week on a Tuesday, in order to give everyone plenty of notice of any changes in advance. However, if you do the timetable on a Thursday because of some unforeseen circumstance, what is likely to happen? If you explain to those involved that there is a delay and the reason for it, then nine times out of ten they will understand. What staff or students do not like are surprises. It is also important to keep this idea of flexibility in mind if somebody (such as a student or staff member) needs you. Don't put off dealing with a student emergency just because today is the day for a certain administrative task.

10. Managing the tasks

Do not spend too long on a task. Keep an eye on the time and set yourself deadlines to complete student administrative tasks. This is particularly important when you are new to the role and you are concentrating, checking and rechecking that you have got things right. Do not lose sight of the fact that people need you, too, so complete a task in a timely fashion and move on. Student administration is only part of your role, crucial as it is. It is good practice at the end of each day and each week to review which tasks you have completed and which ones are being carried over. Check that you have not missed any finer details of a task from earlier in the day before you shut down your computer.

10 things you can expect from technology

Technology in a school is present in several forms and plays a huge part in our working lives. First, there is the technology needed to administer school systems efficiently, such as the school database. We need to consider the skills and training needed for staff who work with our school systems. We also need to consider who is responsible for dealing with any glitches.

Then there is classroom technology. Students have certain expectations about the integral part IT plays in all aspects of our lives, including teaching and learning. School investment in hardware, software and training for teachers is therefore essential. Without training, support and continual monitoring, any investment in hardware or software will be wasted. So, what should we consider and be prepared for where technology is concerned?

1. Resistance

When implementing any new system, you should expect resistance from some teachers and administrative staff. There is often a fear of the unknown, and for teachers there is also the worry that they will not appear competent in front of their students. It is advisable to have a well thought-out, structured plan to present to staff when introducing a change in IT. Include clear and achievable training for staff with individualised goals. Communicate the reason for introducing new technology and, where possible, go as far as to involve them in the decision-making process. In some cases, you may also find resistance among students because, although they might be tech savvy, they may not be familiar with the software and other uses of IT being implemented in the classroom.

2. Problems

Things will go wrong, systems will crash, people will panic, data will be lost. Ensure there are back-up plans in place and invest in IT support that is quick and responsive. In addition, provide clear, easy-to-read troubleshooting guidelines to help deal with common problems. Provide workshops for teaching staff on how to switch from a tech-reliant lesson to a more traditional version, which they will need to do if technology fails. You can also include tips on this in the teacher-induction document.

3. Enthusiasts

Several IT champions will emerge naturally with any new system – those who embrace change and have an interest in technology. This is likely to happen among both the teaching staff and in the administration team, not to mention the student body. Harness this enthusiasm and encourage these people to help others in a focused way. However, do not allow your staff to rely on these 'champions'; instead, make sure that everyone is using the IT provision in the best way possible. Set achievable goals for individuals, particularly those who are struggling to pick up a new system. A buddy system can work very well through technological change.

4. Investment

Technology requires money and time; a package of hardware, software and training is not cheap. Ensure you include all aspects of any new system in your forward projections and strategic business planning. Don't sit still with your investment. Things change, and the cycle of investment in IT is ongoing. Make sure you research what is current and then establish whether it is relevant and necessary to your school. Students will not be impressed by a rickety old smartboard that is slow and prone to freezing.

If your budget does not allow for smart TVs or interactive whiteboards, remember that there are other ways of bringing modern technology into classroom learning. For example, a principled approach to the 'bring your own device' (BYOD) concept will allow students to learn through technology without using expensive school equipment. This will still involve an investment of time (in training), but finances will be relatively unaffected. Encourage a sharing of knowledge of apps and websites among staff.

5. Monitoring

Good IT systems in school and classroom administration help standardise and streamline administrative tasks. Review your systems regularly with the staff who use them to ensure that you are getting the most from the system and that others are able to understand and pick up the tasks easily. Always remember that IT should help not hinder a business. When investing in new IT systems, brief your IT provider as fully as possible on what you want for the school, and also what you don't want. This will pre-empt any future problems. It is, of course, impossible to predict everything in advance, so ensure there is flexibility within any IT system for you to be able to change and adapt it as the school, systems and curriculum grow and change with time.

6. Bad use of time

School IT systems are often remotely accessible. Because of this, it is tempting to work into your evening at home, or when you first wake up. Try not to check work emails continually or to look at documents or the school database. In any case, work that you do late into the evening is likely to be less productive than work you do during the day. It will be more beneficial to recharge your batteries when you are away from the workplace, so try to ensure that you switch off during your downtime.

7. Student expectations

Students often expect to see the presence of technology in the classroom and to learn via this medium. They will sometimes be more technologically literate than their teacher and use jargon that their teacher is not familiar with. Provide practical training for teachers and include ideas and activities in any teachers' handbook or induction document you have. Encourage teachers to keep up to date with new teaching software and give them a safe space to experiment through workshops, observations and peer teaching. Use training sessions to provide them with hints on how to encourage student involvement when using technology. It is important to stress that new teaching software is just another resource to be used and adapted to the needs of the students by the teacher.

8. Lazy teaching

A lack of structure and planning in its introduction can lead to new classroom technology (such as interactive whiteboards) being used in a non-principled way. For example, teachers might be tempted to put on a YouTube clip without setting a task. This is something you would rarely do with a listening or reading lesson, so there should be no difference when using an IWB. There can also be a shift towards more teacher-led teaching, with the teacher in front of the IWB for most of the lesson relying on the interactive screen. In the end it is only another piece of equipment to aid teaching and learning, and should not dominate all activities. Regular discussions, peer-monitoring, mini-observations and guidance with lesson planning can ensure that technology is being used in a principled and relevant way to enhance learning. It is advisable to have a school policy on the use of IT in the classroom that is agreed on and understood by all involved (see Unit 18 on school policies).

9. Product opportunities

With the growing accessibility of technology, there are always opportunities for developing new products. Consider more sophisticated, blended learning course combinations as well as online course delivery. Many organisations will offer at the very least an element of pre- and/or post-course study via a virtual learning environment (VLE). Your IT champions may be able to carry future product developments forward as part of their own CPD. Carry out market research to see what your clients and potential clients may be interested in, and also what your competitors are offering.

10. Risk

Technology brings with it safeguarding issues. Consult relevant statutory bodies regarding data protection laws and safeguarding. Ensure that you have an online and digital communications policy outlining the school view on accepting friend requests on social media from current and ex-students. Set up a school social media page, where students can be directed by individual staff members who receive friend requests on their personal accounts. Consider your policy on WhatsApp groups and the sharing of personal phone numbers among staff and students.

> *"Supporting teachers to use new technologies effectively is essential. Teacher development and training needs to be supported, ongoing and bottom-up – that is, led by teachers themselves – to be effective."*
>
> **Nicky Hockley, Consultants-e**

10 ways of promoting your organisation

Finding out what people need, designing a way of satisfying that need, telling the potential customers about it and delivering it to them, are basic steps for a business. Marketing is involved in most of them. If you work in marketing, you need to be keeping both an inward- and an outward-looking eye on things. Knowing what your competitors are doing, how the market is changing and what future trends are developing are all part of the marketing team's remit. The marketing team also needs to help the operational team with product design, and then develop the communication plan to tell the world about it. It's a combination of good analysis, product development and innovation.

1. **Standard print**
   Despite the massive growth of online marketing and sales, there is still a need for key marketing documents to be printed as hard copies. The courses your school offers, the prices, the dates and references from other students are key information you need to have available. Whenever you are in discussions with a potential customer, employee or supplier, it is good to be able to produce a catalogue, course outline or brochure around which to base the conversation and that you can give them to take away. Allowing the conversation to be driven through the print material allows you to slow down and go over what is important to the person you are talking to rather than just carry on with your sales pitch. The best thing about print promotion material is that it has a life of its own and can be passed on to other people. Posters and flyers are easy to produce and are a useful way of reminding people of your presence, either locally or at conferences.

2. **Website**
   Your website is key to your promotional success because it can grow infinitely and can be updated daily. Don't let it get out of date. There is nothing worse from a marketing perspective than a website with last year's information or a blog that hasn't been updated for a few months. If you no longer offer a particular course, remove the information; if your teaching staff has changed, update the photographs. All your print materials – your application forms, your brochure and your terms and conditions should be downloadable from the website, but again, this should be an easy part of the customer journey. Navigability around the website is crucial, and the more reasons people have to come back to your site the better. Features that are regularly updated, such as blogs about learning and language quizzes, are the best way of encouraging people to come back to your site.

3. **Referrals and word of mouth**
   The best advertising is free and happens through satisfied customers. Their recommendations to others usually cover details about the course that you, as the manager, probably couldn't know – because they are all to do with user reaction. Don't forget that return customers are quite rare in some aspects of teaching because the customer has achieved their personal goal. On the other hand, other family members, friends and colleagues are all potentially new clients, which is why word of mouth is so important. If you are working with international students, it is really helpful to have a student from a particular country recommend your school to others from the same place.

4. The business card

In the words of one of the most memorable advertising campaigns ever: 'Don't leave home without it'. The business card is the encapsulation of key information, the brand and the values for your school. Anyone you meet, either professionally, socially or by chance, is a potential contact for your school, and the easiest way for them to remember you is via the business card. The modern equivalent is the QR code exchange or linking up digitally, but you still have nothing to lose by carrying a few cards in your wallet.

5. Encouraging staff to attend and present at conferences

Everyone on the staff is part of the marketing team without necessarily realising it. Every time they discuss the school or the industry, they are both presenting an image of it and gaining insights into what is going on elsewhere. When staff attend conferences, they need to be proactive and make sure they do actually network, meet new people or cement relationships that the school already has. Those who present are a great advertisement for you as a training organisation, so make sure that some of those costs are included in the marketing budget. When times are hard, as we will discuss later, be careful not to cut back on conferences. They are a vital part of your marketing strategy, if taken seriously.

6. Appointing representatives

Many schools, particularly those seeking to attract international students, appoint and rely on agents to provide customers in return for a commission. This generally works well, provided the agent is working to find new students proactively and not simply acting as a middleman and picking up a 25% bonus for very little work. With the advent of online sales and marketing, and considering the ease with which customers can contact suppliers, the agent has to work even harder for their services to be seen as a worthwhile investment. This 'added value' can come in the form of a genuine knowledge of the target market, which they pass on to the customer in their own language, an ability to offer a range of destinations with travel plans, or good communication skills to deal with a wide range of schools across the world. An agent can also translate all of your sales copy into another language and can explain the finer points in the potential customer's mother tongue.

7. Responding to tenders

Government agencies, ministries and certain companies are obliged to choose suppliers from a shortlist based on quality and price. By responding to a call to tender, a school is pitching for potential future business, but also promoting itself. You might not get the first business you tender for, and you might feel the administrative work necessary was not worth it, but it is worth persisting. It is a way of reaching new students who are currently outside your usual channels – and possibly at times of the year when you need them most. Do remember that most of these calls to tender are published in specific places and you will need to have someone on the staff briefed to keep an eye out for them.

8. **Press and TV**

English language topics often make good news stories which the press and TV like to cover when there is a slow day. Make sure that local media are aware of any events you are holding or even any newsworthy students you are teaching. A 'newsworthy' student might be a local celebrity or someone with an unusual job, age, family background, nationality, etc. Don't forget the value of your own YouTube channel, where you can broadcast events yourself. Short news items and stories make great additions to your web presence. We will look in detail at social media in the next chapter.

9. **Make key decisions about your product**

The best way to promote your school is by thoroughly understanding your products and making the right decisions about them. Customers want to find the product which suits them, but they shouldn't be overwhelmed by the range of choices you offer. How many levels do you want? How many course lengths? How many course types? All of these decisions need to be taken and monitored on a regular basis. Which of your courses make money and how long are those profits enjoyed for? Which are getting stale? Which are the future 'star products'? You are competing with hundreds of other suppliers. What are your unique selling points (USPs)? Can you build on them? You need to know the answers to these questions.

10. **Accreditation and awards**

One final way of promoting your school is by getting official endorsement. This can be through an accreditation scheme or by putting yourself up for awards. Once your competitors know how good you are and are prepared to acknowledge the fact through industry awards, you can use that as strong marketing capital. Accreditation usually involves a lot of preparation and the establishment of certain processes but, again, is usually worthwhile.

"It absolutely essential to develop a deep understanding of your key source markets and the profile of courses most suited to your potential clients from these countries. Listening is a vastly underrated skill in marketing, but unless you ask the right questions and listen carefully to the answers, opportunities will be missed in the way your organization should be branded and presented. Of increasing importance is mastering a clearly thought through digital strategy - combining all aspects of effective online and social media promotion with mobile friendly technology to generate enough enquiries to convert to enrolments."

Andrew Hutchinson, Director, Kings Education,

10 ways of making an impact on a target market

There are so many good schools, so how can you differentiate yourself from the rest? A lot will depend on your situation and whether you are a local school looking for local students or a destination school trying to get more international students. Whatever your situation, marketing never stops, since you need to ensure (or increase) the flow of future students as circumstances evolve. Here are 10 things you can do to make an impact on either your current market or a new one.

1. Being associated with quality

How do we define quality when it comes to a language school? Some answers to this question are globally relevant and others are market-specific, and you will need to adhere to the criteria that are relevant in your particular market. For example, in some contexts, the most important factor might be the qualifications of the teaching staff, but in others it could equally be their professionalism, patience or kindness. It might be that proof of quality comes in the form of accreditation, but it might also be judged in terms of how established you are, how long you've been in business or the kind of references you can supply.

2. Specialise

Your specialisation might come in the form of in the type of courses you offer, such as those for young learners, or those focusing on business English or English for academic purposes. On the other hand, it could be that your location is key, either as a good place to visit, like Oxford or Sydney, or as a place that is popular with a more specific group, such as older students from Japan or *Lord of the Rings* fans. Alternatively, you might choose to offer courses that prepare your students for national English exams or for study-abroad courses. More practically, your school might need to be easy to access before, during or after school or work, or close to a university campus.

3. Success stories

Your success stories are a great way to market your services. A success story might be about an individual student who has done well or a group from a particular branch of industry or region. The where, when, how and how long of their learning journey will make useful advertising copy as it adds real human interest to the dry data of your brochure or fee list. Photos and quotes from happy customers can act as a strong marketing message. They can be posted on a school's website or even within the building as point-of-sale advertising. In a similar vein, any statistics that can be supplied as further evidence of your quality will be useful. The number of different nationalities, your age range or your success rates at various exams are all useful ways of making an impression.

4. Presence

The presence or absence of your organisation at certain key events will impact on your success rate in terms of marketing. You can increase awareness of your brand in various ways, for example sponsoring speakers at conferences, having articles published in magazines such as *English Teaching Professional* and *Modern English Teacher*, or getting into the news based on a case study. A case study might involve describing a particular situation (e.g. a group from a particular place with a particular language level and specific needs) and explaining how your school dealt with it. Being known for good posters, well-thought-out advertising campaigns and useful marketing items (e.g. free, branded water bottles) will also help spread the word about you.

5. Offering teacher-training courses or seminars

By running workshops, seminars or webinars for teachers, you are publicly stating that teaching and learning matter to your organisation. This is an important factor that potential customers will appreciate and you do not have to limit yourself to pedagogic issues. Offering non-academic training courses and webinars (e.g. safeguarding, counselling, sports coaching) can be equally useful because that gives you a chance to assemble your potential customers together with your actual customers offering a great opportunity for word-of-mouth advertising. Encouraging staff to train up in non-language areas can be a useful investment, particularly if they can then help run workshops on these themes. As your school gains new competencies, let your customers and followers on social media know. Such information can often lead to an enquiry call from a potential customer.

6. Being known to teachers

The kind of events mentioned above will help you become known to teachers in the target market. Teachers are a great source of students, whether they are taking a group to your country or recommending your school as the best place in your area to study. Holding open days where you discuss and demonstrate your methodology and materials will also help to make an impact.

7. Social media

Your presence on social media and your use of it give you direct contact with a wide range of potential customers. How you use this opportunity will depend on where you are and what you are hoping to gain but, just as with a website, you will only get out of social media what you put in. Doing it well is time-consuming because you need to be informative, innovative and up to date, whether you are sharing ideas about the language, acting as a forum or promoting new courses. Getting the right balance between occasional posts and regular, interesting information can be difficult until you really understand what you are hoping to achieve. Do remember that once you are active on social media, you need to monitor and respond to any negative posts made about your school.

8. Alumni

It has already been noted that word-of-mouth advertising can be really useful, and in your alumni you have a ready-made source. What can you offer them in return? By offering follow-up services such as online learning or a forum where they can post questions, you are maintaining their customer journey in a useful, cost-effective way while maintaining their goodwill. Former students go on to have important roles in the community and can potentially refer a lot of business to your school. Similarly, if you are trying to break into a new area, such as teaching English to accountants, go back to your alumni and get feedback on how to go about it. Be careful with data protection and make sure former students want to be contacted; if they do, they will be very useful. A simple email outlining your idea and a request for help will usually be welcomed by alumni who had a good experience with you.

9. A strong sense of corporate social responsibility

Having a good reputation in the community will always help in terms of developing your commercial success. Helping the community in ways other than language teaching can also be of great use. This might mean offering special arrangements to certain parts of the community such as the less well off or the elderly, or reaching out in other ways, such as arranging hikes or sports for the local youth. You might choose to be active on an important issue such as recycling, road safety or nutrition. This will not directly generate business but will improve your status in the area.

10. Good people on your team

The final tip for helping to have an impact is to make sure that the people marketing your school are excellent. Your marketing should have the same degree of quality as the services you are providing. You need people who understand the needs of customers and how to match them to the courses you offer in an engaging, persuasive but non-pushy way. Ultimately it is the people you employ to market your school who will have the largest impact on the market. Make sure they are good listeners, and that they are consistent and well trained.

10 ways of networking and using social media

There are numerous ways to network with former customers, current students and potential future course participants. We can stay in touch via social media, email or messaging apps; we know who has visited our websites, how long they stayed there and what they looked at. We also know that by talking face to face we can add value to any relationship we have established; we can do this by attending conferences or meeting and talking to customers in person and in real time. The list below covers five ideas for non-digital networking and five digital ones.

1. **Trade fairs**

    There is something about a good conference that is hard to replicate elsewhere. Whether it is a workshop, an exhibition, a marketing convention or a symposium, it gives you the chance to speak to a large number of your peers and/or potential customers in a controlled way, and is an opportunity that should not be ignored. If you are making a presentation, you have a chance to think aloud, be provocative, show your concerns and offer solutions. It also gives you a reason to invite people, and can be a starting point for any discussions. There is also the added benefit of linking your products to a feel-good experience.

2. **Open days**

    If you want more of the attention to be on your own institution, then open days or familiarisation trips are a good way of doing it. Make sure that the staff are on board and keen to talk to visitors, and that you have a series of interesting things to do, from visits to your classrooms, observations of demo lessons, discussions on areas of development or concern, and opportunities for your potential customers to network with each other.

3. **Outbound visits**

    You cannot always get customers to come to you, particularly if they are based in other countries or cities, so at some point you will have to make visits to touch base, get feedback, discuss future business and so on. It cannot be overstated how valuable these visits are and how seriously they need to be taken in terms of preparation and follow-up. Use the data you have access to in order to get a good idea of who has already been to your school from the market in question and how much they enjoyed it. If there were any issues (and there usually have been), make sure you know what solutions were offered. Return business is generally the easiest to get, but a small issue that was never resolved can often be a reason for someone to go elsewhere. Make sure the possibilities for their going elsewhere are limited.

4. **Chat**

    This can be done in a number of ways. You can pick up the phone and call or you can set up a conference call. You can link it to a particular time of the year or when you have something you want the contact to know about. Whatever the reason, make sure the chat helps develop the relationship, shows your organisation at its best and does not cause any sort of negative feeling. Don't be pushy – it's not a cold sales call, it's a chat between supplier and customer. Keep it simple, but do make sure you do it. It's very easy to push these chats down your list of priorities and then to be surprised when other suppliers start working with your customer.

5. Manage your key clients

When you look at your student numbers and start to analyse where they are coming from, you will notice trends. Those who come regularly to your courses (or those who send people to your school) are your key customers and they have to be treated differently. They should be the people you talk to about launching new products – the ones who get the extra level of service and regular communications from you. On the other hand, be aware of them becoming a drain on your resources and having a negative impact on your bottom line. Key customers do not always have to be offered the best prices; other aspects are more important to them. They want you to solve some of their problems and make their lives easier. Helping them deal with their own customers (where language can be an issue) is a good starting point. Arranging for them to meet each other to discuss the market and current obstacles and issues will also reflect well on your school.

6. Website and social media pages

These have already been mentioned as superb marketing channels, provided your reasons for using them are clear and you have the people with the time to invest in them. Getting a website that people will be happy to spend time on and come back to regularly is an important step which relies on your providing regular new content such as blogs, videos, news posts and so on. You will probably talk to your present and past customers and communicate with future learners through Facebook, Twitter, Instagram, and so on. Remember that the language you use and the points you make should be interesting and non-controversial. Blog posts should always be checked before publishing, as should any comments that people add. The last thing you need is any sort of negativity emanating from your pages.

7. Advertising through social media

The data known about users of certain social media sites allows suppliers to target quite accurately the kind of customers they are looking for. Services such as Google Analytics can tell you the nationalities, professions, age ranges and interests of visitors to your site, and all this data can be put into the mix as you try to identify your future customers. One language school in the UK, for example, targeted students living in towns in Europe near to airports with direct flights to its closest airport in the UK. Given that the flight can often be a substantial part of the cost of a study-abroad programme, this would seem to be a logical use of data.

8. Staying in touch

Social media sites are an excellent means of allowing your students to stay in touch with you and with each other, either before, during or after the course. Something as simple as birthday greetings or remembering a national holiday can help you maintain that relationship with them and they will be the ones who will remember you and recommend you. Allowing them to continue studying online with you or appointing one or two ambassadors among them are both cost-effective ways of marketing through social media.

9. **Keeping in contact with staff**

    You will want to find ways of keeping in contact with staff, particularly if your school's activity is seasonal, or if you are working off-site. Set up a team site or a page on Facebook or WeChat; alternatively, use a team collaboration site like Trello or Basecamp. This is an essential way of maintaining good relations with and among your team: ideas and problems can be posted, materials can be shared, and professional development courses can be offered. It is very easy for teachers to feel isolated when they are only working casually or are new to the school, so a user-friendly, shared site is vital.

10. **Professional networking sites**

    LinkedIn (or its equivalents) is a useful source of ideas and information. Encourage your team to keep their profiles updated – and don't forget your own. Many people search not only for potential staff but also for expertise on LinkedIn: it can be a very useful source of business, an excellent place to post and share professional articles and videos, and a good starting point for your own recruitment needs. Its aim is to link professionals, so take advantage of it.

"One of the challenges of teaching online is that you can feel quite alone sometimes. But it doesn't have to be that way! To keep in touch with my students and the teachers who work with me, I use a mix of tools: Facebook group for students, WhatsApp access for premium clients, a quick Zoom session to check in quickly, Basecamp for managing my team, and face-to-face time to really solidify relationships. When I'm in a big city, I might announce a breakfast or drinks, and any students in that city can come along and meet me & other members of our community. Or I'll travel to meet with my team members in their country. We humans are social animals, and we like to feel connected, whether it's with or without a screen between us."

Christina Rebuffet-Broadus, Creator of Speak English with Christina

10 ways of developing new products

There comes a time in the life of any school when some of the courses being offered start to look a little tired. To pre-empt this situation, it is good practice to evaluate your courses on a regular basis to ensure they still respond to customers' needs, that they are as efficient as they can be, and that they are still appropriately priced. For example, blended learning and flipped classrooms are now part of standard practice, and there have been other developments, such as project-based learning, which have particular requirements and costing methods. In this unit we will look at the steps you need to take to keep your portfolio of products as good as it can be.

1. **Keep a close eye on the market**
   Make sure you know what the other suppliers in your market are offering. At the same time, it is important to know why they are providing those courses, at what price, and whether the courses are proving popular. It might be too late for you to offer exactly the same product, but you might be able to create something similar and better using your own resources, staff and facilities.

2. **Monitor current products**
   Make sure you know exactly how well your own products are doing. Check the profitability and ensure that the gross margin is what you expected. A product that you have been selling for a while might now be underpriced. On the other hand, they should still be good value for money and not excessively expensive compared with the competition. If they are, make sure there are good reasons for this. Most importantly, you need to ensure that they are still fit for purpose, doing what they are supposed to do. If you are running an exam preparation class, make sure the course teaches ways to improve exam performance and doesn't simply practise mock exams. Look at the range of courses and make sure you have the right number for the size of your school, premises and client base. Find out what type of person isn't enrolling and look into the reasons why. This will provide good evidence when justifying an addition to your range.

3. **Analyse product gaps**
   Be aware not only of the learners who study at your school but also all those who choose to go elsewhere. What are the factors that make them opt for another supplier? Think about course dates, hours, extracurricular activities, the profile of your learners and teachers, and your methodology and resources. When you know which learners are not attracted to your courses, think about whether you want to attract them and, if so, what you need to do to get them.

4. **Do market research**
   Market research is not just a case of analysing the market or getting questionnaires answered. It involves the whole product journey from market feedback through to product design and piloting. You probably have learners you can pilot courses on; if not, they are easy to find if you offer the piloting for free. Don't put the course straight into your brochure: trial it and refine it based on feedback from participants and teachers.

5. **Borrow from other sectors**
   Being too inward-looking will prevent you from thinking outside the box and coming up with innovative new products. Look at other sectors, such as hospitality, tourism or conference organisation. What can you learn or borrow from them to ensure a great customer journey? What are the key elements that guarantee a five-star service? Can any of them be transferred across to your school? The success of a school is rarely down to good courses and teachers only, so think of all aspects of the product and where tweaks are needed.

6. **Avoid having too large a range**
   One weakness many schools suffer from is having too many different courses available too often. The net result is that you either end up losing money on courses with too few participants or you start to combine participants into one catch-all kind of course, which is equally unsatisfactory. Someone who has said they need English for exam preparation does not want to be in the same class as someone who needs English for business. They might accept the situation when they are there but they would be unlikely to recommend you to others – and it is well known that negative word of mouth is stronger than positive word of mouth.

7. **Talk to users**
   You can get so many useful insights by consulting learners and teachers. Don't forget that many learners are doing it for the first time and have fresh eyes. Their impressions can be really useful. Similarly, asking your teachers to reflect on the whole customer journey can tease out some very useful ideas which can be used to improve your products.

8. **Use your staff**
   We have already talked about the wide range of backgrounds, experiences and skills you will find on your team. Consult them, use them to develop new products and make sure they are involved in the delivery. So many ideas from primary can be used in tertiary, ideas from large-class teaching can be applied to mini-groups, and elements of once-a-week courses can be used on more intensive programmes. Even though you want new teachers to come on board quickly, you also want them to be critical and to offer ideas from their previous teaching situations.

9. **Achieve the same aims in a different way**
   Fundamentally, the goals for most learners are the same: improve their grammar, vocabulary, pronunciation and skills as much as possible in the time available. So you need to think how you can achieve these same outcomes by different routes. Could things be faster, less stressful, more engaging or better in some other way? One way to make things faster is to use the classroom for activities which require a teacher and encourage other learning to take place outside the classroom. You can also encourage teachers to teach appropriate amounts of language to suit the class, e.g. one or two exponents of a function or the most frequent use of a tense. Language learning can be less stressful when the need for it is obvious to a learner. To achieve this, make sure your teachers teach to the needs of the class as well as the syllabus or coursebook.

10. Think outside the box

To encourage innovation by thinking outside the box, try doing this activity with your staff. In the meeting, divide your staff into four equal groups. Each group is given one of the following key areas and identifies ten points where improvement is needed in the school:

- ▶ your learners
- ▶ your courses
- ▶ your sources
- ▶ your resources.

Groups then rank the ten items from 1 to 10 in terms of importance to the school. They put their results on a large sheet of paper. Display the lists on the wall in four different parts of the room. Groups move around the room and look at each poster for ten minutes. They mark each item as 'ready for review', 'acceptable' or 'getting better'. This will help them judge where the work needs to be done. When each group has looked at each list, discuss how your product range is doing and how it might be improved based on the group's reactions.

> *"When we started our courses for seniors (55+) we only had 3 students. It was a new thing and seniors didn´t know that somewhere out there is an option to learn English in specialised courses. We run on loss first year & invested into marketing. It only started to pay off the second year, after 3 trimesters of loss. Today we have more than 60 seniors and the courses help us covering noon slots for teachers and balance their schedules. Immediate profit is not always the target."*
>
> **Klaudia Bednárová, Director of the Bridge – English Language Centre, Bratislava**

10 ideas you can borrow from other sectors

Sometimes you will have done everything you can to keep your courses well developed and your customers well serviced. If you are still feeling that things could be improved or you are wanting to innovate more, it can be useful to look outside the world of ELT and see what ideas and activities can be borrowed from other sectors.

1. **From the automobile industry**

   Total Quality Management (TQM) is a familiar concept to most automobile companies. It is based on the idea of setting standards so high that the service regularly surpasses the expectations of customers. This in turn leads to an increase in those expectations and subsequently a general increase in standards and continual improvement. It's something ELT can easily borrow from. For it to succeed, TQM is carried out at every single stage as a means of ensuring that the whole process leading up to the final product is as good as possible. All employees are encouraged to look at part of the process and make suggestions for improvement. If this approach is applied to ELT, all stages of the customer journey would need to be quality controlled. The way an enquiry is handled, the paper used for certificates, the type of chairs in the classroom, the reporting system used: each stage of a customer journey would be evaluated; improvements would be suggested, trials done, and then the new approach implemented.

2. **From management consultants**

   Management consultants have a huge range of tools for measuring the key performance indicators of a company. Knowing your business inside out, both in and out of the classroom, allows you to manage much more efficiently. Depending on the situation and the time of year, you could do a Boston Consulting Group Product Matrix, which allows you to judge the potential of your products. You could also do a SWOT or PESTLE analysis, which would allow you to see any opportunities or threats on the horizon. Finally, you can do some basic management accounting to give you a real-time view of how the business is going.

3. **From tourism**

   We all know how stressful travel can be when it goes wrong, and how much we appreciate good service from a tour operator or a travel agent. Both of these sectors were threatened by the arrival of the internet and the increased accessibility of so many destinations to the customer. What successful independent tour operators have added, in terms of value, is a good lesson for ELT. They manage to personalise the whole business by finding out people's needs and then offering the perfect package to satisfy them. Every step of the way is meticulously planned to get it as close to ideal as possible. You often hear about the 'wow factor' in tourism, but not so often in education.

4. **From hotels**

   Hotels have been impacted by the sharing economy, where anyone can let their spare bedroom and have it marketed globally. Hotels have had to fight back by improving their standards, adjusting the offers available and tailoring their offerings to specific markets. Modern digital marketing can help seek out likely potential customers for these packages, and ELT can do the same.

5. From airlines

Airlines have two distinct elements from which ELT could borrow. The way seats are sold and the prices are charged are all worked out by software that ensures that flights are as profitable as possible. In addition to ensuring a good deal for the airline, it also means that the passenger who is prepared to do a bit of research can get a good price, too. The airlines' aim is for the majority of planes to be full, and this is essentially what schools need for their classrooms. Airlines, of course, have blue-chip routes, such as Paris–New York, where they can sell a large number of higher-priced packages in different classes. Schools need to consider what the added value would be if they offered different pricing schemes. To justify higher prices, they can reduce class size, install better technology and furniture or recruit a higher level of teacher. You must decide if the market can sustain these higher prices. Some schools have proved they can.

6. From engineering

The engineering world relies on firms with different specialisations working together. For example, if you want to build a stadium, you will need specialist builders, equipment-leasing companies, transport suppliers, plumbing and drainage specialists, electricians, and so on. The education world also has large contracts; individual institutions cannot possibly deliver these alone, simply because of the huge numbers involved. As part of a larger partnership, however, they would have a role to play. We have already mentioned networking (Unit 22); tendering for contracts is a way of turning those relationships into actual business. An operation of any size can get involved, provided they find the right partners. So look outside ELT for potential partnering possibilities.

7. From retail

Many retail and leisure outlets rely on secret shoppers for feedback on their products and services. Get people to come to your school to take a test or simply get information. Have them join a class as a guest. (You would obviously know the role of your guest but others on the staff wouldn't.) Both of these things will get you valuable feedback on the service you are providing. If you have colleagues in other regions, offer to do the same for them: visit their school as a potential customer and see how good the early part of the customer journey is. Another idea from the retail sector is that of 'pop-ups'. New businesses take on premises on a short-term basis, sometimes within a larger business, as a means of getting their ideas across directly to potential customers. Language schools have even been known to pop up in department stores and on commuter trains. Why not give it a go?

8. From business support groups

By joining local enterprise groups and professional associations, you will start to network with colleagues from other sectors. They can be a great source of ideas for customer retention, local regulations, ways of marketing and advertising, and places where you might find potential customers. Marketing is about building relationships, and working with other businesses in your region or country is a great place to start. It might also lead you to opportunities to tender (see Tip 6 above).

9. **From business media**

Business magazines, books and websites offer a seemingly endless stream of ideas on how to do things better. Even if an idea cannot be borrowed as it is, it can often be tweaked or will act as a stimulus for you to change things in your school. A number of eminent business experts publish regular short articles and blogs. These can act as a great catalyst for stimulating your thought processes. Examples of such resources include *Fast Company*, *Harvard Business Review*, *The Economist*, Forbes.com and Bloomberg.com.

10. **From other sectors**

Think of other sectors that might offer tools, services, marketing strategies or other techniques that you could use in your school. Consider the sectors your students come from or sectors that are important in your region. How can they be of help?

10 financial concepts everyone should know

When it comes to finances, we always seem to divide people into two groups: those who are good with numbers and those who aren't. This is sometimes extended into career choice, classing us as 'financial types' – and then the rest. It is often only when you get to your first management position that you regret not concentrating as much during maths classes at school all those years ago. Do not despair. Getting your head around these ten concepts will see you through most situations.

1. **Cash flow**

   Very much as it sounds, cash flow refers to how money moves in and out of the business. Freelance teachers learn this concept very early on when they are spending money in the first few weeks and are still waiting to be paid. Large organisations who pay an invoice 90 days after receiving it can endanger smaller schools very quickly, as the school will have to pay out for rent and salaries irrespective of whether the client has paid yet. The finance manager must always try to be on top of cash flow and monitor it regularly.

2. **Fixed and variable costs**

   It is often said that a successful business minimises fixed costs and maximises variables. Your fixed costs are items that you have to pay for every month, irrespective of income, such as rent, utilities, certain taxes and permanent staff's salaries. Variable costs will fluctuate depending on your income so, in the case of a school, these might be things like temporary teachers' salaries, the cost of social activities, printing and other teaching resources. Those schools employing teachers on an hourly basis or on zero-hour contracts automatically have the advantage of paying teachers' salaries only when there is student income. The basis of a zero-hour contract is that there is no guarantee of work but, if there is any, those with the zero-hour contracts are entitled to it before any other casual employee. Offering such contracts can make a huge impact on a school's profitability.

3. **Gross and net income**

   As a manager, you will soon see that there can easily be a 40% difference between your gross and your net income, depending on the context. The gross price is the price advertised in the brochure, but any discount or commission offered on this amount will impact on the net income. The net price is therefore what the school actually receives. For example, if a course normally costs $1,000 but the school is giving a 25% commission or discount, then the net income will be only $750. Similarly, there might be a sales tax attached to the price charged, so the $1,000 might include 25% tax. This means that it is actually an $800 course with $200 tax. The school's net income is therefore $800. Your net income is an important key performance indicator and will form part of your management accounts.

4. **Management accounts**

   Keeping an eye on the management accounts, a tool we first looked at in Unit 24, allows you to have a clear idea of how things are going from a financial point of view. Some people prefer to do this monthly and others weekly. Management accounts for a month will include your net income, your key costs (such as teaching salaries) and your fixed costs divided by 12.

This will give you something like this:

Month	Income	Teacher costs	Fixed costs	Result
February	18,000	10,000	12,000	– 4,000
March	22,000	10,000	12,000	0
April	30,000	14,000	12,000	+ 4,000

As you can see from the table, February was not profitable because there was not enough income. The school had salaries to pay and probably not enough teaching hours to offer its contracted teachers. In March, income was higher; the school used the same teachers and managed to break even. By April, student numbers were up and extra teachers were employed. The school was profitable. The ratio of teaching costs to income improved from February to April.

5. Income per class, per week, month or year

Depending on the context, different ways of looking at income will be used. For example, a school that has fixed start dates every month and no off-site teaching is easier to manage than one with multiple start dates, off-site teaching and a number of different modules, each with different weekly hours. If you divide the weekly income by the number of classes being run, you will have the average income per class. This is a useful figure to be aware of when you are deciding whether to open another class or to keep a small class running. As you get used to monitoring these costs, you will find out for yourself which ones are the most important.

6. Teaching costs

In most institutions, the most substantial cost is that of the teachers. Teachers' costs include salaries, paid holiday, sick leave, the cost of covering teachers when they are away, any national employment taxes, and other expenses such as travel, if appropriate. The annual budget will set a percentage for teaching costs. It is usually the most important area to control.

7. Profitability

The management accounts give an indication of how well the school is performing, but it is only at the end of the year, when all income and expenditure are confirmed, that the real results can be confirmed. Profit margin will depend on a large number of factors, but having 10% of the income as profit would be reasonable. As a rule, it is always advisable to try and at least break even: that is the point beyond which things can get difficult quite quickly. Making a loss is an indication that costs are too high for the income being generated. This could be happening despite large student numbers. If this is the case, you need to look at the level of discount you are giving, whether your fees are increasing at the same rate as your other costs, or whether the teaching staff are working fewer hours than they are contracted for.

8. Budget forecasting

At the start of the year the budget is set, setting out expected levels of expenditure and income. As the year goes by, expenditure might need to be reduced (if it is judged that income is not going to make the expected level). Businesses that are very profitable manage to increase budgeted income without increasing budgeted fixed costs. If there is no overrun on the fixed costs, any extra income will be profitable. This is because the only costs involved will be teaching costs.

9. Expenses

Occasionally, staff will have to spend their own money on exceptional items such as travel, meals or materials. As a rule, any justifiable expense can only be reimbursed if there is proof of the purchase in the form of a receipt or an invoice. Staff should always clear it with their manager before making a purchase they wish to be reimbursed for. This avoids unnecessary misunderstandings.

10. Creditors and debtors

At the end of any financial year there will be a number of creditors and debtors. As long as you are going to pay your creditors and be paid by the debtors, the amounts involved will still count in your final profit and loss accounts. When a debt remains unpaid, it becomes 'bad', and will count as a loss in the following year. Unless there is a prior arrangement, it is very important that students do not attend classes when their courses have not been paid for.

"It's amazing how many business leaders don't know the basic metrics of their own company, their breakeven point, their ROI or cost of customer acquisition. Focusing on the key indicators of their business will help managers at all levels make informed decisions, when planning their strategy."

Norman Renshaw, Founder InTuition Languages

10 checks to ensure cost-effectiveness

In any business, the manager is responsible for ensuring that the costs of running the activity are lower than the income. In a good business, the costs are controlled so that the business is run as efficiently as possible and with the quality expected. This means that you need to be aware of, and quick to adjust, a number of variables.

1. Class size

It is often said that a school teaching only one-to-one classes is in a perfect position. They only open a class when there is a student, and so the direct costs of teaching it start and finish with that class. In other schools where groups are taught, the arithmetic is a little more complex due to a range of factors. Many schools offer enrolments on a rolling basis so a class may begin with four students, for example, and rise to say, eight, after two to three weeks. At that point the number may stay at eight but, in certain schools, some students might come to the end of their courses at this point. This means that to calculate the class size you will need to add up the number of students each week and divide the total by the number of weeks. Look at this example.

Week	1	2	3	4	Total
Students	4	6	8	6	24

This class had an average of six (24÷4) students in it over this period. If break-even point was calculated on seven students, then this class is losing money, and might continue to do so. It is essential to know how many students you have per class and what income they are bringing in. Don't forget that the number on the register is not necessarily the number of students in that class for the whole period.

2. Net income per student or per week

When a student pays for a course, there will be a total amount from which taxes, accommodation, materials, enrolment fee, etc. have to be deducted, leaving you with the actual income you will be receiving. That income then needs to be divided across the number of weeks the student is attending their course to arrive at the net income (N) per week. If you divide N by the number of hours (or lessons) attended per week, you will have the data that allows you to see if your classes are breaking even or not. If you work in a school where students pay different amounts, these calculations can become critical.

3. Teaching costs as a percentage of income

We talked in the previous unit about the need to be aware of what percentage of the school's income was being spent on direct teaching costs. Depending on your market, this figure might be anything from 30% to 70%. Once you know your school, you will learn what that figure is and you will need to make sure you can keep direct teaching costs at that level. Increases in that percentage are most often caused by: underusing your teachers (i.e. not giving them the number of hours they are contracted to teach), overstaffing or timetabling inefficiently. For example, if too many teachers are needed at the same time but not at other times, you may end up having to take on extra casual staff.

4. Regular comparing of actual costs to planned costs.

Knowing what percentage of income should be spent on direct teaching costs allows you to track your spending and compare it with what was budgeted. For a school, the budget should be annualised so that you can see clearly which months are expected to be busy (and profitable) and which ones less so. If you have too many lean months with high teaching costs, you are unlikely to make up for that in the better months. Make sure your staffing levels suit the annual profile of your expected income. Think of ways of increasing income in the leaner months by running new programmes or launching new courses for new markets. Think about other languages, other specialisms or other age groups.

5. Analysis of extras

A good school will have a large number of 'extras', which are only required because the majority of the staff are teachers. Depending on your context, there might be travel and travel time, professional development, external qualifications, staff training, parties, social events, materials and subscriptions, which have to be factored in. It is always worthwhile knowing what the real cost of them is, not in order to cut back on them, but in order to have a complete understanding of the real teaching costs.

6. Analysis of discounts

There are many different ELT markets and each of them has a kind of discount typical to that market. In the in-company teaching world, clients often pay for an hour of teaching irrespective of the number of students in the class. As a new year comes around, the customer will want some sort of discount as a reward for their loyalty. This can make it very hard to maintain the income per hour needed to break even. Where schools rely on international inbound students, the market is very much based around agents, who also want a percentage of the fees paid. There is so much competition that it is easy to be tempted to offer an agent large discounts to secure business. In the tertiary sector, there is usually a difference in fees paid by domestic or refugee students and those paid by international students. As such, it is not enough just to count the students; you need to know how much income each one is bringing in.

7. Teaching hours of the management team

Often, some of the best, most experienced teachers a school has are promoted into management positions. If this is happening at your school, it is worth considering whether, across a year, they could be available to teach a certain number of hours. This has three immediate benefits: (1) you keep some key customers happy by putting them with your senior team, (2) your managers keep their hand in in terms of classroom teaching and (3) they can plug any gaps when the school is stretched. Whatever the benefits for you, it will certainly help keep your teaching costs down. You might need to be persuasive to get certain managers to teach, but it is worth it for, say, 150 hours per year.

8. Understanding teachers' contracts

As a new manager, you will become aware, sometimes for the first time, of what actually goes into a teacher's contract. You might also discover that teachers on the same team have very different terms and conditions due to having started at different times. Whatever the contract, you need to ensure that teachers do what they are contracted to do. For example, just teaching one hour per week less than the number the teacher was contracted to teach can add up to at least 40 hours per teacher per year. If ten teachers are underworking by an hour a week, that becomes 400 hours. If, in addition, you have employed part-time teachers, you are essentially paying for those 400 hours twice, and that will impact on your cost-effectiveness and, ultimately, your profitability.

9. Optimising resources

One of the keys to running a successful teaching operation is to optimise your resources. We have shown above how to make sure you get the best from your teaching team, but you have other resources to optimise, too. Think about your classrooms: are they used as much as they can be? Do you have too few or too many? Now consider your online capacity: could you be doing more teaching online and generating some extra revenues? Look at your teaching materials: how much is bought from publishers and how much is made in-house? Could you develop more in-house materials?

10. Balancing old and new customers

Without customers you don't have an operation. Someone once said that an old customer is a bad customer, mainly because they have negotiated themselves into a strong position. There are too many stories of agents and companies who not only have amazing discounts, but also pay so late that they threaten the very existence of their supplier. This is what an old (and bad) customer can do. Make sure they know the value of what you are offering them. In addition, try to keep a good mix of old and new customers: there should always be some future ones being nurtured. That way you should have a balanced income and a secure future.

10 things you can do when times are bad

Whatever sector you are working in, private or public, in-school or offsite, general or academic English, there will be times when student numbers drop, margins decline or costs start to creep up. This is perfectly normal: all institutions go through it and the ones that survive are those that handle the bad times well. Here are some tips for you to bear in mind when things get difficult.

1. Monitor costs

By keeping a close eye on your key percentages during busy periods, you will be able to react in good time if trends start to go the other way. As student numbers drop, you need to adjust the number of classes you are running. However, make sure that you time the closure of a class in a way that is not too damaging to customers and staff. Students who want to continue studying need to have an alternative course offered to them, and teachers who might be coming to the end of an employment period need fair warning in keeping with local employment law.

2. Running loss-making classes

There are times when your judgement will persuade you to keep a loss-making class open. It could be that it is a level you need to keep so that you can feed into other levels later in the year. Or you might simply feel that you should be offering a minimum number of different levels, particularly if you are trying to build or maintain a reputation for quality. Remember that there are always options for converting a group class into a combined course involving individual tuition and self-study. This allows you to maintain a reasonable ratio of income to teaching costs.

3. Vacant classroom space

If there is a downturn in activity that looks as though it might last, it might be sensible to consider other ways of using your vacant classroom space. Is there another activity that you could run there? Is it possible to sublet? For example, another teaching organisation such as a children's nursery or playgroup might be interested in renting classrooms. Should you be thinking about reducing the amount of space you are committed to filling next time your lease renewal comes up? Do the courses you offer make the best use of the space? Discuss all of these issues with your colleagues so that if things do get worse, you are in the best position to cope.

4. Reducing quality

It is very tempting to cut back on certain things when times get hard. By all means look at ways of reducing costs, but only on the provision that they do not unduly impact on quality. Keeping class sets of books (instead of giving them to students) and only using black-and-white photocopies might be ways of reducing costs without impacting on quality. You could also consider using digitally projected content written by your own staff rather than books and other handouts. Provided the teaching approach reflects this change, there would be nothing wrong in making small changes like this to control your costs.

5. Making cuts

This is the natural reaction of financial managers looking to improve the results when things start to look bad. As we saw in Tip 4, it is important to make sure that cuts are not so deep that they impact dramatically on the quality of the product you are currently delivering. Cuts should really be aimed at future activity rather than present – so that you are not impacting negatively on current students. For example, if you decide to change your maximum class size, you can only do that by changing your terms and conditions and your sales literature. One option is to cut back on marketing and promotional activities. Note, though, that while the effect might be a gain on this year's results, there will potentially be a negative impact in the future. Travel is an easy area to cut back on, but if it is in the budget, there is probably a very good reason for it, so consider this option carefully. Look at your courses and analyse where spending is happening. For example, if your welcome pack is expensive to produce and doesn't really offer added value, this is an area where cuts could be made.

6. Inefficiencies

Sometimes a small financial setback can provide you with the opportunity to have a good look at the overheads. The process of establishing where to make cuts is, in fact, a very useful exercise. It allows you to look closely at your activities and establish why things are done the way they are. There might be some regular events that have always happened, but which actually might not be necessary. A particular conference, for example, might have been useful in the past, but no longer has the same effect on your business. Certain trips might be being undertaken every year, when every other year might be just as effective. Staff members might still be carrying out some duties which are no longer useful.

7. Low morale

Make sure that, whatever the level of crisis, you monitor staff morale. It can be easy to exacerbate an already difficult situation by reminding people about it too often. It is important to be clear in explaining the situation, but once is usually enough. Teaching and administrative staff need to be in a positive frame of mind since they are the ones dealing with your current intake of students. Nothing will reduce future numbers faster than a bad atmosphere around the place.

8. Don't overreact or panic

One of the attributes of a good manager and leader is their ability to remain calm, assess the situation and make sensible decisions. This is usually most in evidence when times are hard. Your colleagues will be expecting you to act in a timely fashion, to keep them informed and to make appropriate choices. A downturn in business might lead to several changes – to staffing levels, to the type of courses you run, even to the classrooms you use. Make sure you react to these changes objectively and keep emotions at bay. Remember that the school is there to deliver a service in a reasonably profitable way. As a manager your responsibility is to ensure the school continues to be viable, and this might well mean making decisions that others are not happy with. Provided your decisions aren't knee-jerk reactions, you should be confident about them.

9. Future-proof the business

One of the main roles of the management team is to look forward and plan a strategy that will maximise the potential of the school over the next few years. The best way to avoid seriously hard times is to try and predict what might happen in the future. If you keep an eye on the market, your own KPIs, the competition, world and national events and anything else that will impact on the school, you will be in a better position to preempt any difficult periods.

10. Identify the threats

 Look at the following questions and reflect on how future-proofed your school is.

▶ Are you reliant on a particular source of students? (e.g. nationality, age, agent, key client)
▶ Are any of your courses in decline?
▶ What is the single biggest threat to your future success?
▶ How can this threat be dealt with?

> *"In his book* Banging Your Head Against a Brick Wall, *the artist Banksy writes 'Your mind is working at its best when you're being paranoid.' Paranoia is not perhaps a great state of mind to be in, but preparedness most certainly is. That is what this chapter is all about. By flagging up the challenges that ELT institutions can face and suggesting both pre-emptive strategies and approaches to dealing with issues if they present themselves, it is an excellent and concise guide that managers would do well to familiarise themselves with. Just in case."*
>
> **Christopher Graham, Teacher Educator, London, UK**

10 things your customers expect

By 'customers' we mean all students and staff and anyone else who uses and experiences the services provided by the language school; that can include maintenance staff, visitors, potential customers phoning or emailing, and even the general public passing by your building. All of them will have expectations and hopes for the service they experience. And all of them will provide you with an opportunity to demonstrate your expertise and professionalism.

1. **Minimum expectations**

   All students will have certain expectations about the experience they are signing up for. These expectations will probably differ, especially if you are recruiting from different nationalities and cultures. At the most basic level they will expect an academic environment that is fit for purpose, with learning and teaching facilities and some degree of assessment of their progress. The environment might constitute a building or collection of buildings, or it might exist online. However, some customers may have greater expectations, such as good, fast internet connectivity, a space to eat and relax, a leisure programme, or teachers who are all qualified to a particular level. Because you can't know what all these expectations might be, it is important to state very clearly in all publicity, enrolment documentation and other pre-arrival communications exactly what you are providing. A simple bullet point list will suffice: 'We provide …'.

2. **A clear course programme**

   Your students and other customers may have certain assumptions about what constitutes a learning programme. They may expect the courses to be the same as they have experienced in the past, either in their own compulsory education or in other schools. They may expect a grammar-based approach or a lecture-style delivery or teachers who are bilingual. For younger learners there is the added factor of parents' assumptions and expectations. Take nothing for granted and make sure you spell out the approach and structure of the course: the content of the course, the length of the course, the times of the lessons, the extra work required, the teaching style, the intended outcomes, and, in the case of many schools in English-speaking countries, the fact that students come for different lengths of time (a process known as 'continuous enrolment').

3. **Placement and progress**

   Students will expect to be placed in a class that meets their needs and allows them to make progress in their language learning. The difficulty is knowing what those needs are and how they relate to the needs of the rest of the class. It is not just a question of finding the right level, especially with multilingual classes. Prepare learners for the variety of backgrounds, cultures, experiences and expectations that can be found in a multilingual or multinational class and encourage them to see it as a positive experience in which they will be able to learn from, listen to and support others. Encourage them to see progress not in terms of language they have 'done', but learning outcomes they can demonstrate.

4. Good teachers

Learners always want good teachers, but what constitutes a 'good teacher'? Learners are entitled to expect teachers who are qualified, experienced and approachable. Publicity and pre-course information should give an accurate description of the minimum qualifications held by the teachers and mention some of their qualities (e.g. that they are approachable, patient, professional). Providing some actual profiles of real teachers is a good way of getting this message across, but make sure the profiles you choose are representative of your current staff and that they are kept up to date.

5. Efficient administration

Administrative staff are extremely important to the student experience. They are usually the first point of contact before and on arrival. Students can expect administrative staff to be helpful and friendly, but also to know their job. Not only should the staff themselves be efficient and able to provide quick and satisfactory responses, but so should the information systems and databases they use. Investment in both customer service skills and efficient technology are essential.

6. A comfortable and non-threatening environment

For learning to be effective, students and teachers need to be comfortable and relaxed. This can be partly achieved through physical design and facilities: comfortable desks, a relaxing lounge, posters and plants. But non-physical factors are just as important. All students and staff have the right to an environment that is safe, secure and free from harassment, and this needs to be managed just as much as the comfort of the chairs.

7. Knowing who to talk to if they have a concern

Research shows that the single most important factor for international students is knowing how and where to get help. The roles and job titles of the different members of the academic and administration staff need to be very clear on information boards and in handbooks, ideally with a picture. Avoid complex job descriptions such as 'Quality Assurance and Legal Compliance Administrator'. Instead focus on what they mean for the student, e.g. 'Hi, I'm Luke, I can help you with your accommodation'.

8. Value for money

This is a tricky one, even if your school does not charge fees. All students will have invested time in your school and will expect some return on their investment. You can manage their expectations by clarifying from the start what they can expect (and not expect) from their investment. As part of the monitoring process (for example, at tutorials or one-to-one meetings), you can check that students are satisfied with what they are achieving and are happy with their 'investment'. But you will need to be prepared to offer something, such as a clear explanation, if they say they are not. As a manager, do not forget that your staff have also invested in your school by giving their time and expertise: check that they are happy with their investment too.

9. Making friends

People don't always enroll on a language course solely to improve their language. They may be looking for a new experience, a change in their career path or an escape from a troubled past. Learning a language is one way to meet these aims, because language learning automatically involves communication and contact. Although they may not say it explicitly, many students want to make friends, sometimes lifelong. Many romances and relationships have been forged in language schools – make sure you facilitate and celebrate this aspect of the school.

10. Professionalism

Learners expect professionalism. ELT is an important profession in terms of international communication and understanding. Even if some teachers only see ELT as a short-term job rather than a long-term career, their work should still conform to professional standards. Be proud of your professionalism, and, as a manager, define what makes your provision professional. One useful reflective activity involves asking yourself the following two questions: How would I define 'professionalism'? What are the key features of professionalism? Look at the various services and activities in your school, or a school you know well. Using your answers to these two questions, decide how you could professionalise each part of the operation.

> *"We always ask ourselves: 'How would we expect our own children to be cared for if we sent them to a language school in another country?' This is what every parent is looking for and is at the heart of everything we do."*
>
> **Sarah Tomlinson, Principal, The Isca School of English, Exeter**

10 early stages in the student journey

The term 'customer journey' refers to the complete series of all the experiences that your customers go through when interacting with your organisation. This will include the period before arrival (e.g. when they are considering which school to go to) and after departure (e.g. when they tell others about their experience and when you have any contact with them). Analysis of each individual stage of this journey will involve the understanding and managing of expectations, establishing quality standards and best practice, and measuring the extent to which you achieve them. In this unit we will be focusing primarily on the students, but remember that your staff and any other users of school services are also customers. Note also that the precise stages for each language school will be different because not all schools are the same: the stages considered below are mainly based around an intensive in-country journey but will generally have an equivalent in all schools.

1. I want to learn English

You may think that you do not have much influence over the prospective student's decision to learn English and their choice of school, but you do. Promotion and marketing is the obvious way to attract customers, with direct approaches to your target markets. But you can also use your existing students as recruiters, not only encouraging them to tell their friends and family how wonderful the experience was, but also equipping them with publicity materials and incentives and ensuring they spread the word throughout social media.

2. How do I find out more?

Discerning students (or their parents) will always want to find out more before they commit to enrolment. Although you may not be aware of how they are doing this, as it will often be through user-generated content on advice websites, you can monitor this information and regularly check its accuracy. You can facilitate direct contact through having an easily navigable website and a simple prompt to speak to (or email) someone in person, in the customer's own language if possible. The use of live chat facilities can be effective too. Obviously, staff dealing with direct enquiries should be polite, friendly, knowledgeable and efficient; make sure you monitor interactions to check that this is really happening.

3. How do I enrol?

If the customer is asking this question, you may think your job is done. It's not: they are still only knocking on the door, and they may have other doors waiting. The enrolment process needs to be quick and efficient. Enrolment forms, whether online or offline, should be designed so that they are comprehensive, but also easy to complete, and ideally there should be someone to talk them through it. How well you handle enrolment is crucial to setting the atmosphere for the whole customer journey.

4. I don't know what to expect

Even after the booking has been confirmed and the student is ready to start, there will be further pre-arrival information to communicate to the student in order to explain, for example, how they can get to the school, what they should bring, what will happen on the first day, who they will meet, and where they can get something to eat. You hope the students will be excited and looking forward to their learning adventure, but they will also want to know what's happening.

5. How did my first day go?

The first day at any school is usually busy and confusing. There's a lot happening and the students are in an unfamiliar environment, often surrounded by an unfamiliar language. Where there have been instances of dissatisfaction, it can often be traced back to a badly organised first day. It is worth spending time to get this right with a friendly welcome at the door, clear signage of where to go, a timetable of what will happen, a comfortable place to sit and relax with a coffee, and perhaps most important of all, staff who smile and make eye contact. Treat the new students as your honoured guests!

6. Are my lessons what I expected?

Students have come to learn English. They will expect the learning to start immediately, especially if they are on a short course. Make sure any induction and orientation work you do is delivered in an ELT-friendly style. It is also useful to have introductory lessons on subjects such as 'how we learn/teach', 'what we expect from you' or 'approaches to pronunciation'. These can be delivered while the placement is taking place. Students should finish their first day (or first week if they are on a less intensive course) not only feeling happy, but also feeling they have learnt something.

7. Am I happy with my teachers?

This is perhaps one of the most important questions asked in the customer journey. First impressions count for a lot, and teachers should be briefed to do a good 'PR job' in the early days (and thereafter as well, of course). A confident presence, clear instructions and explanations, and a willingness to listen both collectively and one to one are crucial in order to satisfy the customer and, at the same time, establish the norms for how the teaching/learning will work. Some teachers spend time at the beginning of the course working out a 'learning charter' for students and teachers to adhere to. It is also important to ask the students directly if they are satisfied with the style and outcomes of the lessons.

8. Do I have enough resources to help me?

Students will not only judge their learning experience by the quality of their teachers, but also by the quality of available resources, and the competence of the teachers who use them. They will want to know that the materials are up to date and appropriate to their interests and needs, even if they don't use them much. Instructions on how to use digital media for self-study, VLEs (virtual learning environments) and library resources should be given clearly, but probably not on the first day when there is so much other information to take on board.

9. Have I had an opportunity to give feedback?

Probably the best feedback comes from simply listening to and observing the students in class and in interactions with other student services personnel. But feedback also needs to be seen to be happening at appropriate times, as we shall discuss in the next two units. The student should not only feel they have had the opportunity to give feedback, but also that they have been listened to and that something has been done with it.

10. Will my satisfaction continue?

We have only looked at some of the early stages of the customer journey. Students should expect to be happy with their academic progress and their general well-being right through the course and beyond. The school needs to continue to identify further stages in the journey and assess whether quality standards are being met and exceeded. Use the photocopiable form on page 173 of the Appendix to analyse how well your school manages the different stages of the customer journey.

10 types of feedback

Obtaining feedback on the services provided is one of the main ways in which schools can evaluate and improve their performance. Feedback can be obtained in a variety of ways and for different reasons. It is important to know what the purpose of the feedback is, who it is for and when it is best to gather it. It is also important to have procedures and forms that are easy to complete and analyse, so that high return rates can be achieved and lead to relevant action being taken where necessary. We will explore some of these types of feedback in this unit. Where appropriate we will suggest one or two appropriate questions to ask, but obviously there are many possibilities. In the next two units we will look at what you can do with feedback and how handling complaints can also be a form of feedback.

1. **Initial feedback questionnaire**

   There are certain things you need to check immediately, ideally on day one or two. Depending on the services you provide, you will want to know if the student was met at the airport on time, if their journey to the school was OK, if their accommodation was as expected, if they caught the right bus, and if there is anything they are really not happy about. This can be administered with a very simple form, often requiring a yes/no answer and space for a comment. Alternatively, you may want to ask a short open-ended question in order to check something specific. Examples (related to homestay accommodation):

   Is your accommodation good?

   What did your homestay host give you for dinner last night?

2. **Regular feedback questionnaires**

   Feedback questionnaires can be administered as frequently as you wish, but bear in mind that asking for feedback too frequently can be counter-productive. There are no rules, but once or twice in a 12-week term is probably sufficient, assuming that you have systems in place for issues to be brought up in between. Remember also that long, complex forms tend to be completed less thoughtfully, so ask the questions that you want answers to. A graded response (e.g. 0 to 5) is useful, with space for a comment. You may want to investigate a situation further if someone has responded to a question with a 3 or below, or even if they have 'only' given a 4.

   Examples (related to language progress):

   Do you feel you have made progress in the last month?

   Describe two things you can do now that you couldn't do before.

3. **Online surveys**

   Designing your own online survey using one of the commercial survey applications is a good way of customising the feedback you want to get. But there can be disadvantages: return rates can be lower unless completion is made compulsory in some way; information tends to be numerical and statistical rather than qualitative; the compiler forgets to re-programme the information being sought. Online surveys work best when an organisation wishes to get a bigger picture of how they are doing, rather than address specific points relating to individuals.

4. One-to-one meetings

A direct interview with a student can be a very effective means of gathering feedback, particularly when related to their 'customer journey', but it is of course very time-consuming to do this with every student. You will need to choose individual students carefully, and explain they have not been singled out for any negative reason. It can be useful if, for example, you are concerned that you are not meeting the specific needs of students of a particular nationality. A less intrusive variation of this approach is to trace back the email chain and documentation trail for an individual student and look for any communications that could be improved.

Examples (related to specific nationality needs):

What advice would you give to other [Chinese] students coming to this school?

Is there anything that surprised you about this school?

5. Focus groups

A focus group, as the title suggests, allows you to look in detail at a specific area of your provision and get the views of students. It needs to be prepared carefully, with the students being briefed on the area or areas you want to discuss. It should not be a forum for general complaints and concerns. It needs to be properly minuted with action points being circulated to the focus group participants and, if appropriate, beyond.

Example questions (related to leisure programmes):

Which leisure programme events have you attended in the last two weeks?

Tell us about events that your fellow students think were not successful, and how we can make them better.

6. Student voice

Some LTOs have formal channels for giving students a voice in the operational decisions made. These might come in the form of an elected class representatives or a designated student forum or council. In addition to regular meetings to discuss issues that have arisen, the student representatives provide a quick and direct route for management to access student opinion. Smaller organisations may not be able to sustain a regular student representation system, but can instead offer a regular drop-in session with key staff members or a more anonymous 'suggestions box'.

7. Teacher tutorials

Teachers are a valuable source of feedback, not only from themselves (see Tip 9), but also from students. This can happen informally during lessons and breaks, or more formally during tutorials, which can be weekly, monthly or quarterly; they should always give students the opportunity to express views on issues other than their own academic progress. If this type of communication is not encouraged by managers, students' concerns may simply never be addressed.

Example questions (general):

How are things going for you? Are you happy with everything?

What's your opinion of the new cafeteria?

8. Exit evaluation

Most organisations gather feedback from students at the end of the course, often in return for an end-of-course certificate. It's important to be sure of the purpose of this form and the questions you can usefully ask. Remember that you may not have the chance to respond to an end-of-course feedback form, so think carefully about the questions you ask and, if you want to be able to respond, the day on which you give the final questionnaire. There is nothing worse than finding out that someone was deeply unhappy when they have already left the school, and possibly the country.

Example questions (satisfaction):

How likely are you to recommend our school to other people?

Would you like us to send information about the school and our courses to anyone else who might be interested?

We will discuss what you can do with the feedback in the next unit.

9. Feedback from staff

We have so far focused on student feedback, but remember it is important to get feedback from all stakeholders: teachers, administration staff, ancillary staff, homestay hosts (if you offer accommodation), other managers, and anyone else who might use your services. Regular meetings and appraisals will usually provide this opportunity, but be careful not to overlook it; always ensure feedback is a regular agenda item. Exit interviews can be useful, especially if you are looking to re-employ people in the future.

10. Feedback that meets your needs

There is no one-size-fits-all for feedback. Each school or organisation will have different needs and requirements, defined by the nature of the provision (the courses and services you are offering) and depending on the culture, budget and resources of the school. Taking into account the tips in this unit and using the photocopiable template on page 174 of the Appendix, design feedback forms and systems to meet the needs of your school. If possible, discuss the questions on the template with your management team and produce working documents for your feedback and quality assurance systems.

10 things you can do with feedback

We have looked at various types of feedback and how to ensure they meet different purposes. Gathering and storing feedback in its various forms is one thing, but for feedback to be really meaningful it is important that the results are used in a productive way. The different types of feedback have different purposes, and there are different ways to use each type. In fact, changing the way you use and disseminate feedback can make it more interesting and more likely to be effective. Presenting a similar set of statistics every month can become tedious, so look for different ways to use the information you gather.

1. Don't do nothing!

Surprisingly, many organisations gather feedback but do nothing with it. The people who take this approach may argue that they don't have time to analyse all the information, and that they only need to note major problems; just giving the students an opportunity to express their opinions is sufficient. But what is the point of planting a field with vegetables and not bothering to harvest the crop, or only removing the biggest weeds? If time really is the problem, then just have one simple form to fill in asking questions on satisfaction with basic provision, together with an additional section focusing in more detail on one particular area which you vary each time; for example, teaching and lessons, resources and facilities, extra-curricular activities or safety and welfare.

2. Explain the purpose

Make certain everyone knows why you are asking for feedback and exactly what you will do with it. Explain that feedback requests come in different forms and will cover a range of areas (such as the areas mentioned in Tip 1). Have a clear policy, known to all, outlining your reasons for gathering feedback, explaining how you go about it and describing what you do with it. Make sure you include time frames for responses. Make it clear that, in addition to the various formal feedback procedures, everyone is encouraged to give opinions and raise questions at any time.

3. Deal with the urgent

Identify and deal with any urgent individual issues promptly. For example, if a student says they are very unhappy with the course and are considering leaving early, you need to act quickly and find out what is wrong and what can be done. As with any urgent issue, make sure you contact the people affected quickly (this could be the teacher involved and the student's classmates). Listen to the concern and, if you can't provide an instant fix, set a time frame for when you will get back to the person involved. After you have dealt with the issue, check that the person involved is happy with the outcome, and then record the action you have taken. Dealing with urgent issues is the priority, but don't ignore other comments.

4. Learn from it

It is a natural first reaction to look for negatives and then breathe a sigh of relief that there's nothing to worry about. When there are negative comments or criticisms, there can be a tendency to react defensively with a 'Yes, but …' response. However, the feedback provider may actually have a point. Try not to analyse feedback when you are stressed or in a bad mood, and give your response some time and thought. With a considered analysis, you may find that you are confirming your initial 'Yes, but …' reaction, but you also need to be prepared to learn something new. Don't ignore the feedback that is neither very good nor very bad. Middling comments are also significant and need to be analysed.

5. Pass it on

As a general rule, feedback should be passed on and shared with relevant parties. This can mean simply congratulating a teacher on doing a great job or talking to a member of staff about concerns that have emerged. You can also use feedback to assess how certain departments, teams or groups of staff are performing. However, it is essential to be sensitive, and passing on everything to everyone may not be appropriate. It is best to start by passing it on to the individual; then decide whether you can or should widen it to others.

6. Use it to plan

One of the most useful things about feedback is that it gives you a wealth of information, which you can collate and analyse in order to identify trends, assess performance improvement and prepare forward action. But there is also a danger of too much information, or 'information pollution', as it is sometimes called. Make sure you are getting the information you need, rather than just assembling a multitude of coloured graphs and statistical data. Always ask yourself: Why am I asking for this information? What am I going to do with it? How does it affect our plans?

7. Celebrate it

Good feedback gives you an opportunity to celebrate, individually and collectively. Some organisations have award ceremonies or announce an 'employee of the month'. Rewards can also be given in the form of vouchers, meals out, a half-day off, even a pay rise. Of course, you can also use it in your publicity: on websites, in brochures and on social media. Real student testimonials are effective, but remember you need to get permission from students before you quote them.

8. 'You said, we did'

Don't forget to advertise what you've done in response to feedback. For example, you could put up a poster on the wall that lists what was said and what you did, e.g. 'You said you wanted more water coolers in the building: we've put water coolers on every floor'. 'You said you wanted lessons to start later: we've made the start time 15 minutes later.' Displaying notices like this in communal areas not only tells your students what you have done, but also sends out the message that you are a listening and caring organisation: you actually do something with the feedback forms.

9. **Change the way you do it**

   Feedback can become routine and unexciting, and consequently not very useful. Finding fresh approaches is important. Think about changing the systems and forms that you use, the questions that you ask, the people that you ask, and the way you display or share the results. Varying the approach can throw up different issues and trends.

10. **Do the feedback yourself**

    At an individual level, self-evaluation and giving feedback on your own performance, either through appraisals or observations is a very valuable tool for improving performance (see Unit 37 on pages 117–119). There are also various ways in which an organisation can use feedback systems to evaluate itself and share the findings, in what is sometimes termed 'collective self-evaluation' or 'company self-evaluation'.

Try this activity: get staff individually or collectively to fill in the same feedback forms that are given to students, but rather than giving their own feedback, they predict what they think the students will put, as well as which areas will be seen as strengths and which as weaknesses. The results can be shared and discussed in groups, and then compared with those given by the students. The outcome can be revealing and thought-provoking, sometimes producing a whole new awareness of how the provision is perceived by students.

> "Get feedback from everyone – students and staff, of course, but also from homestay hosts, residence managers, group leaders and agents. Set up systems to ensure that any feedback that needs to be acted upon immediately is seen by the appropriate people, that they record that the feedback has been noted and any action taken. The best overall question to ask is: 'Would you recommend this course to a friend?'"
>
> **Diane Phillips, Inspector, Accreditation UK**

10 tips for dealing with complaints

In business it is often said that over 90% of unhappy customers won't complain to you; they will simply not use your services again. More worryingly, they are likely to tell 10 to 15 friends. It is very likely, however, that even top-quality organisations will receive complaints at some time or other. Sometimes a complaint isn't presented as a complaint, but rather as a suggestion. The line between complaint and suggestion is very hazy, and many managers believe it is best to treat them in the same way, taking them seriously and having thorough and effective procedures for dealing with them.

1. Have a clear complaints procedure

Make sure you have a clear and accessible complaints policy and procedure that is fully available and can be understood by everyone (i.e. with appropriately graded non-legalistic language or in different languages). Most complaints procedures will include: clear information on how to make the complaint (or suggestion), who they should address their complaint to, the format in which to present it, and how they can escalate the complaint if they are still not happy (including to external professional organisations and authorities). There is some evidence to show that the very fact of having a clear complaints procedure that is available and accessible in itself reduces the number of complaints that are actually made.

2. Recognise the complaint

Whether it is a formal complaint (for example, about the quality of teaching) or a serious suggestion (for example, that it would be good to have more comfortable chairs), you need to deal with it promptly. By its very nature, the world of ELT is prone to misunderstandings and miscommunication, either through language difficulties or cultural differences, so ask yourself whether this is just a misunderstanding that can be cleared up by a quick clarification and correction. However, don't jump to this conclusion too quickly. Different cultures and different demographic groups have varying approaches to complaining: some may be quick to complain about anything, others may avoid complaining at all, even when something is seriously wrong. It is worth researching different cultural approaches to complaining, but obviously be wary of stereotyping.

3. Treat it seriously

You should always start from the assumption that the complaint is serious. Do not, for example, be patronising towards the complainant or try to brush it aside (a common reaction when dealing with students with a low level of English). The best way to ensure that you are treating the complaint seriously is to make sure you get all the details. This may take time and effort, and could possibly involve an interpreter, but being fully acquainted with every aspect of the situation will allow you to deal with the complaint to everyone's satisfaction.

4. Have a private place to talk

It is sensible to find a room or a private space with chairs to sit in, and possibly a glass of water on hand. Providing privacy also demonstrates that you are taking the issue seriously. If the conversation does become angry, then it is better that this should happen in a place where others cannot hear. Think about how you arrange the seating: different types of problem may suit different arrangements; for example, across the table if you feel you need to provide objectivity and formality, or side by side if you want a more caring and supportive atmosphere.

5. Listen before you speak

One key skill you will need is to listen and to give the complainant the chance to say what they want to say. Allowing short periods of silence can help to keep the situation calm. The acronym SLAGO is often used in discussions relating to dealing with complaints. It stands for: Stay calm; Listen well; Acknowledge the problem; Get the facts; Offer a solution.

6. Offer a solution

After you have listened to the complainant and gathered all the facts, you will need to explain what you are going to do. You may not be able to offer an immediate solution, but give a time by which you will respond. When you offer the solution, make sure that the complainant has understood exactly what you are going to do (and what you are not going to do). And remember that, in ELT, questions like 'Do you understand?' and 'Have you got that?' are best avoided as checking questions.

7. Training

There are specific skills that you will need to deal with complaints. You may be faced with people who are frustrated, upset, angry and even abusive. You don't need to be a trained counsellor to deal with this, but you do need to have skills for dealing with emotional situations, and it is worth considering getting some formal training. In difficult situations, you should always consider having another person in the room so that any disputed points can be witnessed and confirmed.

8. Keep a record

Always keep notes and details with the time and date of the complaint and its outcome, even if it seemed insignificant and was easily fixed. Not only can you learn from case studies like this, but more importantly you will be able to refer back to the case if need be. Litigation can come months or even years after the incident, and you need to have the facts at your fingertips.

9. Inform people of the outcome

Don't forget to let people know about the outcome and resolution where relevant. Obviously this will be necessary if someone is at fault, but a teacher, for example, might need to know that there has been a problem with a particular student which will require some adjustment to lesson content and classroom layout. Sensitivity is crucial in this case.

10. Learn from it

However troubling or frustrating the experience of a complaint might be, it is important to learn from the experience. You can improve your own performance and that of the school as a whole as a result. Furthermore, you may discover that a complaint handled effectively not only results in a happy customer, but it also gives the customer more confidence in the organisation.

Using the ten questions on page 175 of the Appendix, think about complaints you have handled or made yourself, or that you have been aware of, and complete a form for each one. Include some complaints from outside the world of language teaching.

10 ways of turning 'OK' into 'Wow!'

Some ELT managers are quite happy simply to be assured that the quality of their services are acceptable and meet the requirements of their customers and relevant accreditation schemes. Being 'the best in the business' may not be a goal for them, and they may feel that raising the bar will only lead to more expense and more work. However, we are making the assumption that you want to strive for better quality and continuing improvement. In this unit we present some ways in which you can do this.

1. The 'wow factor'

When did you last say 'Wow!' about anything: a meal, a visit, a holiday, a play, a sports event, an exhibition, a piece of news, and so on? What made it a 'wow'? How did it make you feel? How did you tell others about it? By answering those questions yourself, you should be able to discern the essential ingredients of the 'wow factor'. Look at aspects of your life: where you live, who you live with, what you do at the weekend, your job. Does any of that have the wow factor?

2. Know your USPs

You probably won't be able to wow your students all the time with all your services, so it's a good idea to pinpoint the areas where you think you may already have the wow factor. This could be the experience and excellence of your teachers, the modern state-of-the-art building and classroom facilities, your city centre location, your beautiful garden and outdoor swimming pool. These will be your USPs (unique selling points). Make sure that, as a manager, you know what the USPs of your organisation are. Identify three. Do you promote them effectively in your publicity through text and pictures? Are your staff, students and other customers aware of them? How do you monitor and maintain them?

3. Identify new 'wows'

Quality can be spread. If one section of your operation is doing very well and another is not, analyse the reasons behind this. The weaker section may be able to borrow some ideas, and even some staff who have been successful in building the strong section. To identify areas that would benefit from improvement, look at information gathered from collated feedback forms from students and staff, especially if you have a graded scale of scores. Establish an area that has 'wow potential' and focus on that for a period of, say, three months.

4. Use accreditation criteria

All accreditation schemes, such as the Accreditation UK (British Council) Scheme and EAQUALS, will have criteria against which performance is measured. They will often specify what is needed to meet minimum requirements and what is needed to demonstrate a strength. Use these criteria to evaluate your school. Again, this procedure can involve all staff members or just managers, as you prefer. There is an increasing trend for accreditation schemes to request self-evaluation, and the scheme will also often indicate what constitutes 'a need for improvement' or 'a strength'.

5. Ask!

Sometimes you can be too close to your product (in this case, language teaching and associated services) to see where the 'wow' opportunities might come from. So get ideas from everyone: students, teachers, administration staff, agents, your own family and friends, people visiting the school or those just passing by. Many of the resulting ideas may be unworkable, but occasionally there might be a gem. Treat each suggestion seriously (for example, ask yourself whether it would work, what it would cost, and who could lead it).

6. Launch a quality campaign

Start a campaign to promote quality across the school, involving all students, staff and stakeholders. Display posters around the school with definitions, quotations and questions, such as: 'What is quality?' or 'How can we be better?' Dedicate a wall in the common room for students to post examples of good quality within and beyond the LTO. Make 'quality' a theme or a topic in the learning curriculum.

7. Awards and prizes

Find out about awards and competitions that are available within the ELT and general educational sectors, and also within the local area (e.g. local enterprise awards). Even if you don't win, preparing an entry for an award will give you a focus for achieving excellence. If you do win an award, it will not only give your school a sense of pride, but will also provide a wonderful marketing tool.

8. Give a score

The practice of setting targets and giving scores in educational management has not always been well received. However, it can be an effective way of analysing and improving performance. For each stage of the student journey (e.g. answering an enquiry, the 'day one' experience, dealing with a complaint) or each operational area (e.g. recruitment, safeguarding, measuring learner progress), give a score out of ten for how your organisation performs, where 'five' is the minimum expectation. You might find it easier to write each point as a 'quality standard' (e.g. 'All students will be welcomed by a member of staff on their first day', 'Students are placed in classes appropriate to their level and needs') or, alternatively, you could take one of the responsibilities listed on a job description (e.g. 'to deal appropriately with students who have poor attendance'). If you wish, you can involve the whole school in this scoring exercise, but it is important to come up with a series of numbers to work with – as we shall see in Tip 9.

9. Raise the bar

Once you have the established scores, you can work to improve quality and set targets. It doesn't actually matter what those scores are; it's all about incremental improvement. Having established minimum quality standards for each stage of the student journey or each operational area, set up working parties from within your organisation to decide how you can exceed those expectations; in other words, how you can move from a six to a seven, or even to a ten (but remember that improvement might be gradual). Going the extra mile might involve offering students a welcome drink on arrival, a free vocabulary book, or free use of a gym. You could do the exercise on your own, but it is good to involve others.

10. **Ten things we want to improve in our school**

Select ten quality standards for areas you want to focus on for improvement in your school. The list could include a range of areas such as better teaching of pronunciation, a more exciting colour scheme in the school, a digital upgrade of the SMS (school management system), more accessible and exciting noticeboard displays, and so on. Work on them all over a specified time frame of, say, 12 weeks, and then select the top three most improved areas for gold, silver and bronze awards. The photocopiable table on page 176 of the Appendix will help you do this and gives some examples of possible quality standards (as mentioned in Tip 8), but try to come up with standards that are relevant to your school.

> *"I learnt early on in my career when a student complains about something – a class being too easy, for example – not to take it personally and become defensive but to act to resolve the issue. Listening is important but effective action is even more so."*
>
> **Heather Daldry ELT consultant, UK**

Unit 33

10 points to remember when planning a new course

The curriculum is the backbone of your organisation. It is the set of courses or subjects that make up a possible course of study. The courses you offer may evolve organically with changing demand. It is important to keep abreast of what others are offering and to monitor your course provision. There are certain things that you should consider when introducing new courses or, indeed, a completely new curriculum.

1. Curriculum fit

It is essential to consider where your proposed new course fits into the existing curriculum. Is the addition an obvious one or are you expanding into a new market? Consider how this change fits with the vision of the organisation. It is important to know your existing product in order to do this: ask yourself what the USPs of your curriculum are and how a new course will enhance this.

2. Market research

It is important to know what your competitors are offering, but do not be solely dictated by this consideration when introducing a new course. Know what is evolving in the industry and how your curriculum can meet the changes. Do research with all your stakeholders. Carry out structured focus groups and short surveys with existing students, partners, staff and alumni.

3. Timeline

Do not assume that introducing a new course is a quick and easy thing to do; it involves detailed planning. Map out your plan for the introduction of the new course clearly in advance. Choose your team to carry out research, write publicity copy, write the course content, source materials, etc., consider staff workload and make space to dedicate time to introducing a new course. If you are the course developer, ensure you have the time and resources to do the job well. It is advisable to set SMART (specific, measurable, achievable, realistic and time-bound) goals when working out your timeline. Nominate one person to monitor the progress of the goals.

4. Costings

Part of the planning procedure involved in setting up a new course involves looking at the costs. Consider set-up costs and factor in the hidden costs, such as staff time. Consider costings with the bigger spending picture in mind; for example, think about whether the course will take away income from other courses. Also consider your running costs and take time to calculate both pessimistic and optimistic projected numbers. A rule of thumb is that you will not see a return on investment on a new product for up to two years. Is your organisation able to absorb this?

5. Enthusiasm and expertise

Look at your existing staff and consider whether there is an appetite for this new product. Are they enthusiastic? The staff who will be delivering the course may not embrace the change, or they may not have the expertise. This should not stand in your way of meeting market demands, but you do need to think about how you get your team behind the new course. If necessary, you will have to provide training so that the new venture can be seen as a positive change by otherwise unchallenged teachers who are familiar with the current curriculum. Alternatively, you may consider a recruitment drive. It is also important that there is enthusiasm and subject knowledge in your administration and sales teams.

6. Planning the course itself

There are certain logistical steps to follow when planning the design of the new course. First, draw up a syllabus – an overview of what you want to include. In order to do this, the learning outcomes of the course should be clearly defined. From here, draft a skeleton plan of the main course elements to be covered and how and when they are going to appear in the course. Consider the learning outcomes of each section. Do they meet the main aims of the overall course? Share your draft plan, get feedback from others, review and update. Finally, add substance to the plan in the way of materials and lesson planning ideas.

7. Pilot

Once you have the initial components of your new product, it is important to trial parts in isolation, and also to pilot the whole course. Be open to different types of delivery. Will the course involve blended or distance learning, for example? Developing a new course is an opportunity to extend modes of delivery. Get feedback from students and the teachers trialling the course. In order for this to be effective, teachers should complete a course review form (see page 177 of the Appendix for an example of such a form), and there should be slots within the course description for teachers to make notes as they deliver. They should comment on what worked and what could have gone better. Analyse the feedback received and make changes as necessary. Repeat the process. Any course plan is a working document and should be reviewed regularly; however, a new course will need particular fine-tuning.

8. Promotion

When you are introducing a new course or relaunching a revamped curriculum, it is important to let everyone know. Promotion is key to making it a success and you only have one chance to make a first impression. Get the marketing team on board, provide sufficient training and guidance on how to launch this in the best possible way. Identify the key selling points, tell all partners, advertise it on social media, write a blog about it, do a press release, even hold an event or offer a promotion. Tap into the loyalty of your current student body. They will all have friends, work colleagues and family members who may be interested to learn more, especially if it is linked to a loyalty promotion such as 'introduce a friend'.

9. **Lifespan**

   Once details of the course have been published, it is important to run it, regardless of how few students sign up in first few months. Cancelling a course gives a bad impression and makes potential students wary of signing up to others. Be prepared for it to run at a loss to start with. However, it is also important to review the success of a course or any other change to the curriculum. Don't get too attached to a course you have been personally involved in, keeping it running when it is serving no purpose. Anyone can get things wrong, and market demand changes, so be prepared to drop a course or to introduce an alternative. Equally, be confident and expand when you feel the time is right.

10. **Analyse your current curriculum**

    Student demand dictates the courses we offer. When was the last time you did an honest and thorough analysis of your curriculum? Arrange focus groups or surveys with your existing students and partners to gauge what sort of interest there is in new courses. Very often a new product is so obvious we don't see it. Or it may be that an existing product only requires the smallest change to re-energise it. For example, introducing a blended element to a course rather than talking about 'homework' can bring a new, updated flavour to a course.

> *"Always start at the end of the course and work backwards. It sounds counter-intuitive but if you start with the end goal(s), you are able to reverse engineer the language and skills that are needed, and when they are needed, to build a coherent course taking students from where they are now to where they need to be."*
>
> **Emma Bentley, Director of the English Language Centre, University of Liverpool**

10 principles behind timetable planning

Every school will have a timetable of classes which may have started as a small document and which has grown organically, with courses and times being added on along the way. The timetable will be unique to each organisation, and should clearly reflect such complexities as off-site courses, intensive courses and zigzag schedules (where classes run on alternate mornings and afternoons to allow two sets of courses to run in your school, thus maximising the use of the premises). Ensuring that the timetable is clear and accurate and that it is utilising staff efficiently is a skill that all academic managers must master. Inaccuracies made in producing the course timetable, whether it be weekly or term-based, can lead to frustrated students and staff, not to mention possible financial losses to the school. Here are 10 principles to consider when timetable planning. They assume that there is already a timetable in place.

1. Transparency and clarity

The timetable should reflect what is in your publicity and on your website. The publicity document (your brochure or website) may highlight information such as the maximum and actual number of students in a class or the number of teachers teaching on a course. Make sure you stick to these numbers as this is what the client expects and signed up to. The timetable should be a clear, self-explanatory document, where everyone involved can find the information they require. With this in mind, if last-minute changes are made, be sure to communicate these to the people who need to know.

2. Financially viable

It is a very fine balancing act running the correct number of classes and levels to match your student profile, while ensuring that you reach your break-even point. As the number of students changes, it is crucial to monitor the number of classes you have, and to know when to merge, close or open a class. The academic manager will have a clear idea, day by day, of how many spaces there are in each class. If necessary, they will be able to suggest moving a weak or a strong student appropriately to balance the numbers, all the while keeping students at an appropriate level.

3. Below the break-even point

Don't be afraid to open a course that has a number of students below the break-even point. Some specialist courses attract a niche market of students and are good for the school profile. They are also eye-catching for your partners and potential students. Such courses also benefit a developing teaching staff and keep them motivated. There are a number of reasons for running small classes: trialling a new type of course, meeting the demand of existing clients or moving into a new market. In timetable planning, ensure that you know why these courses are on your timetable; avoid running courses just because you always have. In order to meet your overall break-even point, your 'cash cow' courses should carry the extra load.

4. Timetable as a CPD tool

Your timetable is your biggest asset in teacher development, so be aware of this in all the timetabling choices you make. Updating the timetable should not be treated as a simple admin task. Instead, careful consideration should be given to which teachers will teach which courses. Where there is more than one teacher on a course, think about which teachers will work well together. Do not shy away from opening a course simply because you have resistance from staff; instead; put appropriate training and support in place for them. Open the classes you need to open to meet customer demand, and work with teachers to ensure they are confident enough to deliver on the course.

5. The practicalities

Whether you update your timetable once a term or once a week, it is important to have a system. This system will vary from organisation to organisation. Start from student numbers, number of classes and levels. Make changes, merges and closures as necessary, and communicate these changes to everyone involved well in advance and in various forms. For example, put the updated timetable on your school noticeboard, but also email or speak to those who need to know about the changes. Avoid making changes for the sake of making changes and communicate your reasons to those affected.

6. Communication

Consider how to provide timetable information to students. If your database allows you to print individual student timetables, do this including level, room number, teacher name, name of book (if you use one), etc. If this is not possible, provide a written copy where possible and check that the student understands everything. Where a student is moving from one course to another, provide them with written and verbal details of this move. Remember to inform both teachers.

7. Staffing

Ensure that your timetable and staffing projections correlate. It is an ongoing job of an academic manager to monitor student numbers and project how many teachers are needed. Depending on your context, this will be more or less straightforward. For example, where you have continuous enrolment every week or every month, student numbers will fluctuate. Look for peaks and troughs in student numbers, plan your staffing accordingly and do not become complacent. Be prepared to lose teachers as numbers drop and hire as numbers rise. The more forward-planning and building of goodwill with the teachers the better. What you must avoid is having too many teachers and running at a loss. Equally, you should avoid finding yourself in a situation where you are unable to open classes because you do not have enough staff.

8. Flexibility

Once you have finalised the timetable for the coming term or week, stay open to change. There may be a sudden surge in numbers or a demand for a one-to-one course. Accommodate this demand whenever possible – even once you have finalised your timetable. Remember: timetabling is not merely an administration task to be completed then shelved. With this in mind, it is important to build up plenty of goodwill among teachers so that you have teachers you can hire or put on hold as demand dictates.

9. Review your system

It is useful to question whether your timetable is still working to full capacity for the good of the school and the students. Any organisation can fall into the trap of doing something the same way for years. For example, small timetable changes could make all the difference. Ask yourself whether 9am is still the best time for your morning class to start. Would 9.15 be better so that students avoid the rush hour? Could you introduce classes in the quiet times of day to utilise your building and provide extra work for teachers? Before making any big changes to your timetable, do your research and explore all the possible consequences of any change.

10. Review your own timetable

Find a peer who is not familiar with the timetabling system and the work that goes into it. Explain your timetable to them and describe how you approach updating it. Include every detail. Ask for comments on the procedure and suggestions for improvements. A fresh pair of eyes can often bring new ideas to a long-standing system. Use this reflective exercise to remind yourself of the best practice you put in place and to consider any changes to the process you might make.

'In my experience, both teachers and students thrive in a context defined in the short term by stability and continuity, and in the longer term by variety and change. Planning and preparing timetables should be treated as a creative endeavour and is, I believe, a task best approached as a balancing act between these two, contrasting, imperatives. Students need to be exposed to a variety of teaching styles and methods, so pay attention to each student's prior learning experiences. Teachers, of whatever degree of experience, need to be presented with a range of levels and their concomitant challenges, so refer to the developmental objectives agreed in your team members' last Annual Appraisals and the feedback from their developmental observations. Whether working within fixed terms of study or continuous enrolment, the art of crafting a timetable is one of balancing stasis and change (and always having a plan B).'

Danny Carroll, Director of Studies, Kings London (Kings Education)

10 ways of ensuring and measuring student progress

The main reason students are studying with us is to improve their language level, perhaps for future studies, career, or for social reasons such as travel or communication with their extended family. They expect to see real progress. We owe it to them and to our profession to ensure that optimum progress is made and measured, while also equipping them with the tools to continue learning once they leave us. It is also important to manage student expectations as students will often arrive in a language school with an unrealistic idea of how much progress they will make. In this unit we will look at ways of ensuring that progress is being made.

1. Progress tests

The most common way of measuring progress is to test what has been taught. This can be done on a regular basis, possibly weekly, monthly or mid-term. The result allows the teacher and academic manager to see what has been learned and where more work is needed. It also allows for ongoing individualised course planning. Finally, it is rewarding for the student to see where they have improved and what areas they should be working on. A progress test should contain no surprises and should not be designed to catch students out. It should check students' knowledge of what has been covered in previous classes rather than testing a deeper knowledge of English. You may decide to have a set of standard progress tests designed by the academic manager, or you may decide that tests should be set by the teacher. Whichever way, a progress test should be short and to the point.

2. Tutorials

Student tutorials go hand in hand with regular progress tests. These can be five- or ten-minute one-to-one meetings with the teacher or academic manager, held on a regular basis. They can open up discussion on where and how a student can improve, and they allow the participants to agree on a set of learning goals to work on until the next tutorial. For tutorials to be effective the student and teacher or academic manager should follow specific guidelines. Check general well-being, too. If a student is not happy with another aspect of their time with you, this will impact on their studies and progress. See page 178 of the Appendix for a set of example questions you could ask in a tutorial, as well as a student progress review form you can use.

3. Setting goals

Training students to set SMART (specific, measurable, achievable, realistic and time-bound) learning goals will enhance, and allow you to measure, progress. A goal will be effective only if there is 'buy-in' from the student and guidance from the teacher. We can make goals SMARTER by adding 'enjoyable' and 'reviewed'. If a goal is set but not reviewed, the student is likely to lose enthusiasm. On the other hand, if they see their goals being achieved throughout the course, they will be in a better position to set their own learning agenda in the future.

4. Teacher feedback

When done in a thorough and focused way, regular feedback from the teacher to the students on their progress can help to ensure ongoing progress in learning. Different ways of providing feedback and really stretching students in every activity they do will enhance learning. Teachers should be made be aware that the use of well-thought-out feedback at all stages of the lesson is a powerful tool and should therefore run through all aspects of teaching and learning. Include a training session on this in your calendar and provide guidelines in your induction document. Factor teacher–student feedback into teacher observations and into the feedback you give to the teacher.

5. Homework

The work that a teacher sets for students outside the classroom will reflect where progress is being made very clearly for both student and teacher. It allows the teacher to see what has been learnt and what still needs more classroom attention. Homework may take the form of a task where language introduced in class is used or explored in more detail. For example, asking the students to research a topic and plan a two-minute presentation allows the teacher to see if the language of presentations has been absorbed. Homework may also be used in a more traditional way to consolidate what has been taught in recent classes through some form of exercise or activity. Finally, it could take the form of flipped learning, where the learning and studying are set as a task to be completed outside the classroom in order for students to bring their new-found knowledge into the classroom as a place of experimentation and deeper learning with teacher guidance.

6. External exams

There are a multitude of external English language exams available for students to take. Working towards an exam can be motivating for students and working through the levels is a way of clearly measuring progress. It is often the role of the academic manager to advise on which exams may be suitable for students. The academic manager must ensure the student is being realistic about the level of exam they wish to take, and they should provide appropriate guidance, perhaps including an examination preparation course, to ensure that the student makes the progress needed to pass the exam. In order to provide expert advice, you and your team must have a clear knowledge of the criteria for the different exams and an awareness of their validity, reliability, moderation and proficiency. There is a lot of support available for students and schools from examination boards, so be sure to tap into their resources.

7. Student feedback

Arrange focus groups with students to allow them to reflect on their progress and the goals they have set and achieved. Students in the midst of a course are often not aware of how much progress they are making, so encourage them to reflect on how far they have come and what they can now achieve linguistically. See page 179 of the Appendix for an example of the type of form you might use in this process.

8. Repetition

Test–teach–test is a sure way to measure progress from one lesson to the next or even in the space of one lesson. An extension of this is to encourage students to revisit their entrance test or to re-do activities and exercises that they have done previously. They will see clear progress immediately. There may be occasions when a student does not show progress in a particular area. This is not a bad thing, and should be seen as an opportunity by the teacher and student to work on what strategies are needed to advance to the next level. We all plateau at times in our learning.

9. Observation

Regular and focused classroom observation by the academic manager will provide an outside and expert pair of eyes to see where group and individual progress is being made, and where additional work could be done to aid progress. If a teacher is unsure about the progress of their group, they might like to invite the academic manager into a class to provide extra guidance.

10. Record keeping and data analysis

Make a record of progress-test results, monitor goals that have been set, and ensure they are being achieved. Review pass rates of external exams and compare them with any entrance or mock tests that were set beforehand. Review progress on the whole as a school. Are students generally progressing at an acceptable rate? It is the role of the academic management team to review and draw conclusions, and to set action points based on an analysis of such records. Students expect to see quantifiable progress and we need to ensure we can show them this in the form of solid data.

> *"In my school to ensure student's success, we use exit tickets, which is a technique to show you what students are thinking and what they have learned at the end of a lesson. Should a student fail his exit ticket, he re-sits it again. It's an ongoing assessment."*
>
> **Ms. Maha Hilmy, British School Principal, Advanced Education, Cairo Egypt.**

10 ways of improving the quality of teaching

A good learning organisation should not become complacent when teaching and learning seems to be running smoothly. The quality of teaching should be regularly monitored, and mechanisms should be in place for continual improvement of overall teaching standards and of individual teaching skills and delivery. This will keep you ahead of your competitors and allow you to deliver the best service to your students. What follows are 10 ways of improving the quality of teaching.

1. **Recruitment**

    Know where there are gaps in your teaching team's ability and recruit appropriately. It may be that there are trends in teaching that a new member of staff can bring to the team. New energy in the teaching team can lead to existing staff members finding a renewed passion, and this in itself will often improve the quality of delivery. Make it clear in your job advert (as well as the job description and person specification) that an interest in developing and growing as a teacher is essential. This will ensure that you get the right people. See Unit 15 for further tips on effective recruitment.

2. **Values and vision**

    Have a clear strategic focus and defined academic standards; these should be agreed, known and adhered to by staff. Review them regularly with your academic team and ensure that they are being implemented to the highest level. With the teaching team, agree on an organisation-wide teaching action plan at least annually. Your set values might include details of quality, customer care, respect for all stakeholders, dedication to professional development and commercial viability.

3. **Teacher support and development**

    It is important to keep in mind the necessity for individualisation of professional development in order to enhance the teaching performance of each of your teachers. This should clearly sit alongside the organisation-wide action plan or academic vision. Classroom observations and student feedback provide a good insight into areas where improvement is needed in teaching provision. Ideas relating to professional development are covered in more detail in Units 41 to 43.

4. **Resources**

    Ensure your resources are up to date and relevant to students' learning and classroom practice. Remember to monitor both published materials and IT hardware and software. However, doing this alone is not enough. Teachers must be aware of what is available and how best to use the materials and resources to meet the ever-changing needs of their students. They should be enthusiastic about experimenting with the resources available and sharing ideas with their peers. Create 'teacher champions' (people you identify as keen and able in a specific area) to feed back on various resources. They should also have the respect of others; this will allow them to help others and get their peers on board with any new developments being introduced. Teachers may also need reminding of how best to use the old favourites in different ways.

5. **Data**

    Most organisations collect student and staff feedback in a number of ways (see Unit 30). Make sure this feedback is actually being critically analysed over time and that it is used to improve the quality of teaching. Look for patterns by analysing student feedback forms. With staff, look at why less than satisfactory patterns might have emerged and discuss how these can be addressed. Gather data from external examination results and set targets to improve pass rates. Form a 'quality committee' made up of staff from a number of departments, and possibly also students, to analyse and provide their own perspective on the data. Allow them to propose areas for and means of improvement.

6. **An integral approach to teacher development**

    Professional development (PD) should be an integral part of the organisation, running through all systems: recruitment, the teaching timetable, appraisals, observations and student feedback. As a manager, it is easy to treat professional development as an add-on to other tasks. However, for it to successfully improve teaching standards and enhance staff motivation, it must underpin all decisions an academic manager makes. For example, make sure you know when a relatively inexperienced teacher is ready to teach an examination class; then provide them with support and constructive feedback; then analyse the results of the course. Doing this is often just as important to improving a teacher's quality and range of teaching as encouraging them to attend an external workshop. Make this clear to staff and show them where PD exists and how it happens within the school system (i.e. ensure they understand that it is not just delivery of workshops). Show your team evidence that positive results of PD initiatives (such as teachers achieving their goals) have an impact on positive student feedback and that in turn can lead to an improvement in exam results.

7. **Remember the students**

    Students should be at the heart of any plans and strategies for improving the quality of teaching. It is great if teachers are able to implement the current trends in ELT, but only if doing so is going to benefit their particular learners. Ensure that both the school and individual teachers are aware of students' needs. Introduce a system whereby teachers use and revisit student needs analyses to set learning outcomes and related teaching goals. To be successful, this practice must be monitored, reviewed and linked to student feedback and progress results by the academic manager.

8. **Peer and group training**

    Create a sense of collaboration within the staff room. A good developmental way of doing this is to set up small working groups of three or four teachers working over an agreed time period on an area of development they personally want to improve on. The area of development chosen should tie in with the developmental vision of the school. The working groups decide on common teaching improvement goals, research to be done, peer observations and the collection of student feedback on the area of interest. The role of the academic manager is to guide the teams through their project where necessary, but not to provide extensive input. At the end of the project, the groups present their findings to the rest of the teaching team, complete with evidence of what has been learned and how the results have impacted on teaching practice and student feedback.

9. Learner autonomy for teachers

Encourage staff to take responsibility for their own development in line with the vision of the school. As we equip students with the tools to continue learning a language without the need for a teacher to be present at all times, we should do the same for teachers in their professional development. This is achieved through awareness-raising, and by providing the space, resources and guidance for teachers to recognise where to focus in terms of improving and enhancing the quality of their teaching. Set up regular performance and development meetings with teachers to guide them in achieving their goals. These can take the form of short 10–15 minute meetings to review annual goals, progress so far, and how to break long-term goals into smaller, achievable steps. Encourage staff to use one of the various apps or platforms available for recording one's own CPD. Alternatively, set up your own in-house system. See pages 180 and 181 of the Appendix for an example form with instructions that you could use to record a teacher's CPD.

10. Deciding on teaching standards

Do you have a set of standards for the delivery of teaching? If so, how do you monitor and measure what goes on in your school to ensure they are maintained and improved upon? Set up two or three meetings with a focus group of staff to agree on a set of standards. Share these with the wider teaching staff and agree as a team on ways of checking, through key performance indicators, that the standards are being upheld. You may wish to use criteria set by an inspection body such as EQUALS or the British Council Accreditation Unit. Alternatively, you could use guidelines provided by a local quality assurance organisation.

"The ultimate goal of improving the quality of teaching is to enhance learning which in turn impacts the learner's experience and the school's success academically. Therefore, investing time and money in this area as a school is crucial. However, no observation or training is effective if a teacher doesn't have the intention or the motivation to do so. It is up to us as managers to be role-models and enable teachers, so that a culture of delivering quality teaching is not only achieved but also maintained."

Shanel Summers, Ex Academic Manager of Wimbledon School of English

10 ways of doing lesson observations

Classroom observations are a vital tool in any ELT organisation. Used effectively, they ensure that quality standards are maintained and that teachers are able to develop. For them to be successful it is important to have a clear policy and procedure, understood and agreed by all. If the recruitment and induction procedures have been carried out effectively, then classroom observations can focus on initial and regular quality assurance. Even more importantly, they allow the teacher to develop in line with the standards and direction of the school, and to the benefit of the students.

1. Formal quality-control observation

Observing a teacher fairly soon after recruitment and then regularly as part of your quality measures is a common and useful system. Don't set your teacher up to fail but give them a chance to demonstrate their teaching skills. Have a clear procedure to ensure that both teacher and observer know their roles. Ensure at least one goal is set to give the teacher something concrete to work on, for example: 'Aim to personalise your activities to the interests of the students rather than just following the exercises in the coursebook' or: 'Make sure you use students' names when asking open questions in class to ensure activities are not dominated by one or two students'. Keep a record of the classroom observation including a copy of the lesson plan. These records can be used to feed into the bigger developmental picture for the individual teacher and as part of the school developmental programme. (It is also useful, and often a requirement, to have such documentation available for external school inspections.) See page 182 of the Appendix for areas to focus on when doing teacher observations.

2. Focus, honesty and empathy

Put yourself in the teacher's shoes. If we can make observations as stress-free as possible, the results will be far more positive. This will lead to greater willingness from teachers to embrace different types of observations, leading to an open-door approach to classroom observation. When you are delivering feedback, it is important that you base it on evidence, rather than making subjective judgements on style or personality. Do not shy away from areas that you feel require further development, but give teachers the chance to recognise these for themselves first. Remember to provide a focus for further development and improved classroom skills in the summary statement at the end of your observation notes.

3. Ten-minute observation

Short observations are beneficial for a number of reasons. If you have a large or spread-out staff to observe over a number of sites, make your initial observation ten minutes long. This will be enough to give you a first impression. If necessary, you can follow up with longer observations on lessons where you feel immediate remedial work should be done. Ten-minute peer observations are always good at induction stage to allow new staff to get an impression of the 'house style'. You may choose to do a 'learning walk', where you observe each class for ten minutes unannounced on the same day to allow you to get a snapshot of what teaching and learning looks like in your school at any one time. For a learning walk to be focused and therefore beneficial, concentrate on one aspect of teaching and learning. For example, you could focus on teachers' use of the board or the use and frequency of concept questions.

4. Blind observation

This is where a lesson is planned and then delivered in the absence of the observer; the 'observer' is available as a guide and a focus to allow the teacher to talk through the lesson both beforehand and afterwards. In order for the blind observation to be successful, the manager must work with the teacher to schedule a time for the lesson to take place. As manager, you should ensure that a lesson is being prepared in advance, with consideration being given to the learner outcomes and anticipated problems, i.e. that the observation is being taken seriously. An appointment for feedback is arranged to take place shortly after the lesson has taken place. This is a space for guided reflection, where the teacher talks through the lesson with the 'observer'. Blind observations work well when there is structure to them. If a passing suggestion is made that a teacher try a particular technique 'at some point', and they are not given a date to try it or a scheduled follow-up, they are unlikely to take it seriously.

5. Filmed or recorded observation

Having teachers film or record themselves provides a good alternative to having someone observe during the lesson. Ensure that teachers have access to the necessary equipment (e.g. a camera or audio recorder) and that they know how to set it up. Alternatively, it can easily be done using a smartphone. Either part or all of the lesson can be filmed. The camera can be focused on the teacher or on the students (with their prior consent, of course). Video is helpful for observing such aspects of the lesson as instruction-giving, group dynamics and boardwork. It also allows the teacher to see how the students react to the various stages of a lesson and to observe things they may have missed during real-time delivery. You could also just audio-record the lesson. This is easy to do on a smart device. This allows the observation to focus on such aspects of the lesson as the use of pronunciation, effective drilling and the use of the teacher's voice. After the lesson, a teacher can watch or listen either alone or together with their manager. If you are watching with the teacher, help them to draw conclusions and make plans for development based on your and their observations.

6. Evidence-based observation

Here, feedback and conclusions are based solely on the evidence of what is happening in the lesson. Evidence-based observations are much more objective and fact-based than traditional ones, and as a result they are often more readily accepted by the teacher. For example, in a traditional observation the observer may make comments such as, 'There is a nice rapport. I like your approach to …. Some of the students didn't seem engaged'. In the case of an evidence-based observation, the observer agrees with the teacher beforehand on three or four areas of classroom teaching to focus on during the observation. Draw up a chart to record these various points (see the example on page 183 of the Appendix). Your role is to gather evidence and then present it back to the teacher in order to facilitate discussion around the findings. Evidence-based observations are good for experienced teachers who want to analyse their teaching style and skills in detail. Note, though, that in any observation there should be a sufficient amount of evidence-based feedback.

7. Peer observation

A peer observation system can bond a teaching team and lead to a greater appreciation of each other's work, thus creating a more open-door atmosphere in a school. Involve the teaching team in compiling a procedure and set of guidelines for peer observers and those being observed to ensure 'buy-in'. A common problem in setting up a peer-observation system is the timetable. Teachers may be teaching at the same time. If this is the case, think creatively. An alternative is to provide a timetable of team-teaching slots rather than passive peer observations. You can also arrange a peer observation timetable using filmed, recorded or blind observation methods instead of the traditional peer observation. The keys to the success of a peer observation system are that (1) there should be no threat or judgement to the teacher being observed, (2) there should be a time to reflect and, very importantly, (3) the manager should draw up a clear timetable to allow the observations and follow-up meetings to take place.

8. Action research

Action research goes one step further than a standalone observation. It allows an experienced or long-term teacher the freedom to explore an area of teaching and learning that they would like to develop more through observation and research. As with any developmental project, the academic manager must be able to provide the structure, guidance, support and means for this to be successful. When done well, action research will benefit the students, but it will also reinvigorate a stagnant teacher; it can even lead the teacher to widen their research in the form of an MA, or to prepare a presentation for an international conference, for example. See page 184 of the Appendix for a basic outline of an action research project.

9. Observing underperformance

When a teacher is underperforming, begin by finding out the reason, if possible. Then consider how you can provide support and put instant remedial guidance in place. When observing, consider two or three crucial areas to focus on and provide a Performance Improvement Plan (PIP; see page 168 for an example). Be honest but not harsh. This experience can be stressful for a teacher, so a combination of observations and developmental guidance sessions is often the most helpful solution.

10. Student observations

The one observer who is always present is, of course, the student. Revisit your feedback processes to ensure they allow you to get the information you need on lessons, as perceived by the student. Hold focus groups with students and encourage teachers to get honest and constructive verbal feedback from students. With teachers, discuss ways in which they might act on student feedback.

10 tips for effective appraisals

The performance appraisal is a tool used in management to reflect on, evaluate and future-plan a staff member's performance and contribution to an organisation. It is often measured against a set of organisational standards or values. It consists of a regular meeting, normally annually but sometimes more often, between an employee and a line manager. These meetings are sometimes daunting for both parties but, done well and with adequate planning, they are very effective in boosting morale and getting the most from a staff member. In most teaching organisations there is little opportunity for promotion; it is crucial therefore that appraisals offer some concrete developmental incentive. What follows are a number of tips to help you ensure that the appraisals you carry out are effective.

1. Fit for purpose

If your organisation has an appraisal system in place, review it in its entirety to assess whether it is serving a purpose or whether it is merely a routine activity that all staff go through in the same way each year. If you do not have an appraisal system, do some research and decide on the desired aims, structure, framework and guidelines of your appraisal system. An appraisal should be a way of reflecting on achievements and contributions, along with setting out a continued future path of goals for the coming year. This should be linked to the bigger mission, values and vision of the organisation. (See page 185 of the Appendix for some suggested appraisal questions.)

2. Staff training

The appraisal system will only be successful if all staff are aware of its aims and purpose. Provide adequate and regular training for line managers who carry out appraisals and discuss how to deal with potentially challenging areas or members of staff. Equally, ensure that all staff are aware of the purpose of the appraisal and know how to prepare in advance in order to gain the most benefit from it. It should be a positive meeting with no surprises. With the correct training and preparation, each appraisal should be a positive time of reflection and discussion leading to an agreed action plan for the coming year and a clear set of guidelines on how to achieve this.

3. The appraiser's role

The appraiser's main role during an appraisal is to listen objectively and to guide the appraisee to reflect on their performance and development path within the organisation. Listen with openness and do not interrupt or put words in the appraisee's mouth. Ask open-ended questions and request concrete examples; remember this is their time. Do, however, ensure that you keep the meeting on track. Do not let it unfold into a critique of the school. This is about the staff member; the onus is on the individual's performance, not the school's performance.

4. The appraisee's role

This is a prime opportunity for the appraisee to really reflect on their work and achievements over the past year. It is also a platform to discuss future plans and seek support and guidance from the school. Allow them ample notice to prepare and emphasise the value of such a meeting. Provide them with the appraisal template and their job description and, if necessary, remind them of the outcomes of the previous appraisal. The appraisee should ensure that they have allowed enough time to attend the meeting without it feeling rushed.

5. Preparation

In order for an appraisal meeting to be effective, it is crucial that both parties prepare in advance. Set a time and place for the meeting and make the framework accessible to the appraisee beforehand, encouraging the preparation to be given serious thought. It is a valuable exercise on professional reflection. Once a date has been agreed, avoid postponing, where at all possible, as this belittles the importance of the system and it will therefore not be taken so seriously. When preparing, make sure you think back over the duration of the time since the last appraisal. It is easy to remember and address only the most recent areas of performance. Both parties should make notes in advance, but the actual meeting is a dialogue where the notes are merely an aid to be referred to during the meeting and then revisited and rewritten post-meeting. If you expect a meeting to be difficult, rehearse what you want to say in advance. Try to anticipate points that may be raised for discussion by the appraisee and think about how you would respond.

6. Surprises

Appraisals are not the place to deal with poor performance issues for the first time. Doing this will not achieve anything positive. Any issues should be addressed and recorded as they occur. On the other hand, don't shy away from addressing any performance issues that have occurred throughout the year, making reference to the plans that were put in in place to make improvements. An appraisal should be a fair and honest account of the year and not merely a feel-good, congratulatory meeting. It is important that both excellent performance and less satisfactory performance should be documented. Although you, as manager, should not surprise the appraisee, be prepared for the appraisee themselves to bring surprises to the meeting. If this happens and you do not know how to respond, suggest that this point should be revisited in a later follow-up meeting, and, of course, do make a point of following it up.

7. Goal-setting and follow-up

One of the main outcomes of an appraisal is that a set of goals beneficial to individual and the organisation are agreed on. Goals should come from the appraisee, so encourage this as part of your preparation for the meeting. It is also useful for you as the appraiser to have an idea of some goals you could suggest, based on the teacher's past performance, their areas of interest, and growth areas in the school. Try to make the goals as robust as possible to ensure they can be realised. It is usually advisable to set no more than three, if they are to be fully achieved. Do not then allow the goals to remain unaddressed until the next appraisal. It is the line manager's role to ensure throughout the year, or before the next meeting, that each goal is broken down into manageable stages and that the individual is given support to reach them.

8. Practicalities

Set an appraisal calendar for yourself for the year. Without this there may be a tendency to fall behind in scheduling meetings and for staff to fail to reach goals and targets that have been set. If an employee does not have a regular performance review, they might soon start to feel undervalued. If you manage a large team, it's a good idea to collate a 'goals' document so you can keep on top of helping staff members achieve their goals throughout the year. After each appraisal meeting, do the paperwork promptly while the discussion is still fresh in your mind. Otherwise, the final part of the process becomes a chore. Ensure that the finished summary is signed by both parties.

9. Performance-related pay

Some appraisal systems are linked to performance-related pay, a system that is often held up as a motivating way to reward staff and to encourage them to perform to the best of their ability. If you decide to pursue this approach, particularly in a teaching context, ensure that you have very clearly defined KPIs (key performance indicators), and that you have transparent evidence of the levels of achievement for each KPI. See Unit 40, Tip 6, for more on KPIs.

10. Lead by example

Who monitors the line manager's performance? Just as you work with teachers on their appraisals, you too may have an appraisal with your own line manager. If so, share a brief summary of your goals and achievements with your staff. Show them that you are also progressing and developing. This will encourage them to have a greater belief in you as their manager and it will add value to the appraisal system.

One approach is to introduce a means for you to receive feedback and suggestions from all the departments you engage with and manage. Plan carefully to ensure that you ask the right questions and know how to respond to the feedback in a constructive way. This strategy can be very rewarding but it can also be quite sensitive, so talk it through first with your line manager or even a critical friend. Note that staff members may not be happy to add their names to this feedback, so it is advisable to keep it anonymous. Start by asking a couple of simple questions such as, 'What do I do that you find useful?' 'What could I do more/less of in my role?'

10 ways of monitoring and rewarding staff performance

We should never take staff loyalty and hard work for granted. With this in mind, it is important that managers notice dedication and excellent staff performance and reward it appropriately. This leads to strong staff morale and a build-up of goodwill, which may need to be called upon at certain times. Not all rewards need to be costly to the organisation. The little things we do to show recognition go a long way.

1. Acknowledge success

The obvious and possibly most personal way to reward staff performance is to take the time to acknowledge it. Provide targeted and meaningful positive feedback when someone has performed well or gone the extra mile. Flag it up, tell others and thank staff in general for their hard work. This can be as simple as remembering to take the person aside to thank them personally for their efforts or sending an email round to let everyone know about the achievement of their colleague.

2. Memorable moments

A good way to reward staff is to surprise them with something. It could be as small as suggesting they leave work an hour early in recognition of how hard they have worked that week, getting ice creams for everyone on the first hot day, or organising a team treat such as afternoon tea or lunch: something that makes them say 'Wow, I'm glad I work here'. Use key periods to create these special moments, for example at the end of term, at the start of term, when a contract has been won, or when a project has been completed.

3. Show off

Encourage staff members to share their achievements, possibly in a staff meeting, newsletter or social media. This could come in the form of a regular departmental news slot to allow other staff to recognise the good work that is happening and others' personal work achievements. Outside your organisation, seek out publicity by placing an article about your staff performance and achievements in an industry or local publication. Some organisations have a 'staff member of the month'. If you decide to use this incentive system, the 'winner' should not be decided by senior managers but by colleagues; otherwise, it could lead to bad feeling and accusations of favouritism. Agree on criteria and establish how the staff member is to be chosen.

4. Opportunities

Recognise and reward performance by identifying strengths in members of staff and providing new opportunities. For example, a teacher may have been particularly good at running impromptu CPD workshops and generally helping others. Why not ask them to present a workshop at a teachers' conference such as IATEFL or TESOL, or to sign up to run a webinar for a local teachers' organisation? Or a staff member may have been using their rusty French to help low-level French speakers in their free time. Offer them a free online French course.

5. **Challenge**

    A powerful way of rewarding someone is to encourage them to take on a project or position of responsibility: something that will give them a new challenge and motivation. Ensure that this new challenge is interesting and check that they would like to pursue it; otherwise it will not be a reward. Invest in the staff member and provide the space, guidance and resources to achieve this new challenge.

6. **Monetary rewards**

    You may decide to offer performance-related bonuses to staff. It is important to have KPIs (key performance indicators) that everyone has agreed to for this to work. Consider carefully how you implement this and how you manage disappointment, too, as not everyone will receive a performance-related bonus. You may also decide to provide an all-staff or departmental bonus for a successful project, a good inspection result, a contract won, or even for a successful year. For this to have meaning, it is important to make clear the reason for the bonus. Once bonuses start to be given as a matter of habit, they no longer constitute a reward; rather, people start to expect them. Another possible financial incentive is PRP (profit-related pay). This can work successfully but must be given a lot of consideration. Consider in detail how the profits will be divided or how you will deal with disappointment in years where there is no profit. Think about how you will explain to staff that investment sometimes comes before profit.

7. **Other staff rewards**

    Days off or additional leave are alternative ways to reward staff performance. This incurs a cost to the organisation but it can be considered as an alternative to a bonus. Vouchers for a favourite shop or theatre, cinema and discounts at the local gym are some other ways of providing a one-off reward. Many local businesses will be open to providing a promotional discount to staff from other local businesses.

8. **Promotion**

    You may notice a natural progression in a staff member's performance to the extent that they appear to be moving towards a higher position of responsibility. At this stage, review your team. Is there a logical space for a new position? Approach the staff member and suggest they put themselves forward for promotion to a more senior role.

9. **All-staff reward**

    Do something for your staff 'just because you can', and because you want to show your gratitude for their loyalty, hard work and dedication. You might arrange to close the school and give everyone a half-day off. This is a big decision and it should not be taken lightly. Think through the impact on any classes that would normally be running over that period and establish how you will make up the time. Could you and the other senior managers cover the work while the staff enjoy a reward? Alternatively, throw a party to say thank you or arrange an all-staff day out at the weekend.

10. **Monitoring staff performance**

    In order to reward performance you must first monitor, notice and measure excellent staff performance. It is important to be fair to all. Think of five or six ways you could do this, for example through quantifying and measuring student feedback. See page 187 of the Appendix for some suggestions to help you with this.

10 ways of encouraging professional development for teachers

Although professional development (referred to as PD, continuous professional development or CPD) is widely considered to be important, there will be times when staff do not want or feel the need to engage in any professional development. This may be due to complacency, particularly in the case of long-term staff, or the transient nature of seasonal staff. It is important to note that a good manager will recognise that not everyone in the team needs to be pursuing development goals all the time. There may be times due to personal circumstances, or even CPD fatigue, when it is okay to just be doing a good job. Here are 10 suggestions for ways of encouraging professional development.

1. Know your staff

A good manager should know what makes each member of their team tick – what motivates and interests them. You should know their teaching style and also be aware of what is happening in their personal life that may have an impact on their performance and commitment to CPD at this moment. Only once this is achieved can you help them to play to their strengths and tap into their professional development potential and aspirations. In order to get to know your staff, take time to talk to them in a personal as well as a professional capacity.

2. PD culture

It is important to ensure on an ongoing basis that there is a culture of meaningful professional development, which is embraced by all staff. Highlight the PD opportunities you provide for staff as a perk of the job, a benefit to working for your organisation as opposed to a competitor's one. Make it clear from the start that staff members' willingness to engage in professional development is also an expectation of the school – and show that you invest accordingly. Highlight PD as an enjoyable and integral part of everyone's role within the school. Involve everyone and show that it is taken seriously. This approach should run through everything from recruitment to observation to appraisals, to exam results and student feedback. Do an informal check from time to time by being around your staff to see what is being talked about in the staffroom: are discussions about teaching and lessons taking place? Is there an atmosphere of general positive energy? If so, you are doing something right in creating a positive CPD culture.

3. Individualisation

Professional development is not only about attending a programme of workshops. In knowing your staff and their individual areas of interest you will be able to identify, for example, who might develop best by taking on an action research project, who would prefer to identify an area of development and learn through structured peer observations, and who is ready to get involved in course development. Agree on individual goals that fit in with the school development plan, then help facilitate these along the way.

4. Reflective practice

Create a culture of professional reflection, allowing staff to recognise how they have developed. They might think about the positive impact it has had on the quality of their working life, and also on any student feedback they receive and how much progress their classes have made. Reflection can be done in a number of ways: keeping an online journal or CPD record (see Unit 37 for an example), sharing thoughts with a peer partner, making small and frequent reflective notes on a specific area of focus throughout lessons, and reviewing all these on a weekly basis. Reflections should go beyond simple descriptions (e.g. 'This is what I did'); they should be evaluative, analysing what has been learned as a result. Highlight to teachers the benefits of reflection. Emphasise the fact that this does not need to be a time-consuming chore; instead it should be an integrated and enjoyable part of our working lives.

5. Peer and group work

Peer partners or small working groups can be about much more than peer observations. Allow such groups to evolve organically with the guidance of the line manager. Peers or small groups can identify an area of interest that they can do research on, experiment with, plan together, peer-observe and reflect on. This gives teachers autonomy, and is a more bottom-up approach, with them being in control of their own PD. In order for this to be successful, it must be planned for, embraced by staff and given time and resources. It works well when time is an issue. Make it a final goal to share findings and achievements with peers and, where possible, with students.

6. Tap into the new

New teachers can invigorate a complacent staff, so it is important to tap into this energy. Teachers straight from initial training courses, from other schools, or straight from diploma courses will have a bank of ideas and information about current trends in ELT. They will also have an enthusiasm for their new job and are often eager to share their new-found knowledge. You can tap into this in a number of ways, for example in the form of staff workshops or, more informally, by encouraging them to share ideas with colleagues in the staffroom or to write an article in the school newsletter. Alternatively, long-term teachers may be keen to do some peer observations of newer teachers to get some fresh ideas. Such enthusiasm and idea-sharing is contagious and can spark a renewed interest in PD throughout the school. (See also Unit 38.)

7. Pitch

Professional development opportunities within a school will only be taken seriously if they are pitched at the correct level. In the same way as in a classroom environment, where you would rarely mix all levels of language ability, try to group teachers more or less according to needs when running workshops. Consider your audience: is the content suitable, relevant, too basic or too complex for the teachers attending? If workshops are teacher-led, make sure that the session leader has pitched the content appropriately. Get feedback from staff after workshops and adapt accordingly for future events.

8. **Rewards and incentives**

   Good professional development is rewarding in itself and creates a sense of achievement, especially when the teacher can see obvious progress and results from their efforts. But it is also a good idea to give staff the opportunity to showcase their PD work to the broader industry as part of their bigger PD plans. Encourage them to write an article or to speak at an international conference such as TESOL or at a local teaching event. An opportunity to travel and share the knowledge gained from PD goals can be a nice incentive for the teacher, and is also good for the reputation of the school.

9. **Lead by example**

   A good manager will have a set of developmental goals to work towards as well. Do not end up being so busy that you forget about your own PD. Share this with your team and involve them where possible. Ask for feedback on the progress of your goals and projects. You may decide to focus on an aspect of management or an aspect of teaching and learning that you can trickle down to staff with confidence. You will benefit from this, as will your team, but you are also sending a strong message that PD is important to everyone in the organisation.

10. **Professional development opportunities**

    There are more ways to tap into professional development opportunities than just attending workshops. Think of five to ten other ways to help develop staff. See page 188 of the Appendix for a list of suggestions. Think about which of these might be successful for each individual staff member on your team and how you might introduce it. How will you monitor the success?

> *"Professional Development (PD) is about learning something new and being able to do it. However, oftentimes, teachers do not receive any kind of support in implementing the new ideas. This comes from traditional conceptions of PD but we must realize and start to acknowledge that PD is something to be done with teachers and not to teachers."*
>
> **Gabriel Diaz Maggioli, Ludus Center, The Catholic University, Montevideo, Uruguay**

10 ways to ensure professional development achieves something

One of the key areas that can make your school stand out from the competition, and one that will make teachers want to work there, is good professional development. Poor professional development, on the other hand, is often perceived as a patronising waste of valuable time that could be more usefully employed. So how do you ensure that your professional development achieves useful results for the school and the staff? Read on as we offer 10 tips.

1. **Be prepared**

   Make sure that the PD is well prepared and well thought out, and that it will help all the teachers to perform better in the classroom. This means linking your observations to the PD programme as well as responding to areas requested by teachers. PD should, ideally, be short and sweet, and should fit in to all teachers' availability. For this reason you might decide to run a series of workshops multiple times so that everyone can attend at a time that suits them. It's best to have participants who are keen to be there and not in a hurry to leave to teach elsewhere. You can also run different sessions for different groups of teachers depending on either their experience, the level they are teaching or the type of course they are running.

2. **Be up to date**

   Invest time in the preparation so that sessions are well researched and up to date. The person leading the session needs time to prepare – probably two to three days for a good workshop – so this has to be factored in. Offer some pre-sessional reading rather than relying on eliciting ideas from participants cold during the session. Make sure that there is always a takeaway that they can use in their teaching. This could be an activity to try out, a new technique to test, or a piece of classroom research. Make sure that anything you notice in observations that stems directly from a PD session gets noted and talked about. This shows the practical and immediate usage of development sessions.

3. **Be democratic**

   Encourage as many of the staff as possible to run occasional sessions so that there is not a feeling of top-down communication. If sessions can be based around classroom research, there is more data to build into them and the points being made will have added validity. If those sessions can be turned into conference sessions or journal articles, then so much the better.

4. **Reserve the time and honour it**

   Ensure that PD is taken seriously by advertising the programme in advance and insisting that nothing should get in the way. No teaching or other meetings should be allowed to cause the postponement of a PD session. Make sure the room is perfectly set up, just as you would for external participants, and that there are well-produced handouts if appropriate.

5. Teach them what they need to know

Adopt a test–teach–test approach to the particular area of development. Find out what teachers know, input some new material and then find out how the session has helped them. You can use KWL charts (see page 189 of the Appendix), where teachers make a list in one column of everything they know about a topic (K), a list of what they want to know in the second column (W) and at the end of the session they can complete the third column with what they have learnt (L).

6. Goals and milestones

All staff members should, as part of their annual appraisal, set learning goals for themselves at the start of the year. These goals need to be monitored throughout the year with milestones set up. A teacher who wants to improve their materials writing could do some research on the topic, pilot their own materials with their class, run a workshop with some colleagues as a 'show and tell' and finally have the materials used and commented on by some colleagues. Each of these steps should be recorded, and lessons should be learnt along the way. Teachers might wish to keep a journal of their reflections or use some of the commercially available PD software such as MyCPD, an online tool that enables you to log and track your professional development, reading and research. The tool is free to use and you can upload documents and photos, and add personal reflections, including how what you have learnt might impact your subsequent lessons. See www.etprofessional.com/mycpd or www.modernenglishteacher.com/mycpd for more information.

7. Expect improvements

An investment in PD should result in things getting better. This could be measurable if, for example, you have been working on a particular level or course type. Exam results might improve or the number of students re-enrolling might go up. Other improvements might be less tangible, for example there might be an increase in teachers' confidence or a better atmosphere around the school. Monitor the improvements and comment on them to the relevant people.

8. Action research

If staff have been doing action research, you will want to see the results. How has the research helped the school and its students generally? Was the research for in-house use or can it be used on a broader scale by being published or presented at conferences? Is there any possibility of funding for future research? One of the things schools can do is close the gap between teaching practitioners' insights and applied linguists' more academic research.

9. Review regularly

A semester of PD should be reviewed by the management team and other stakeholders. Is the PD useful to sales and marketing teams in terms of highlighting the pedagogic values at the core of the school? Are there areas of non-pedagogic PD that would be useful, such as sessions on soft skills, critical thinking or counselling, or maybe ones on other areas of the business such as health and safety? Is the PD of genuine use to the school? If not, then it will need to be reconfigured. Sometimes the approach will need to be changed as the population of the staff changes or, in some cases, because the staff hasn't changed.

10. Plan PD sessions together

 Get together with a group of teachers and plan a series of ten PD sessions. Look at the sessions you have chosen and discuss the following questions:

- ▶ Why is this topic important?
- ▶ Who knows about this topic?
- ▶ What more do we need to know?
- ▶ How can we research it?
- ▶ What would be the impact on our classes?
- ▶ Who would be the best person to run it?
- ▶ What would be the best delivery method? Workshop? Flipped classroom? Report on research?
- ▶ How will we follow up?

"Professional Development should be an organisation-wide practice and not just limited to teaching staff. It is vital that all staff are given opportunities to develop and progress. It's about establishing a culture of collaborative learning and improvement throughout the whole school."

Varinder Ünlü, Principal, Speak Up London

10 ideas for managing your own professional development

Professional development includes you as a manager. Apart from the benefits to your team, the students and the school, you will feel a greater sense of achievement and job satisfaction if you are working towards developmental goals. It can be easy in the busy life of a manager to forget about this aspect of your work. However, it is crucial to your own well-being at work that you make PD an integral part of your work, too, in order to keep you fresh and motivated, not to mention respected by your peers and team. Here are 10 ideas for managing your own PD without involving an extra workload or added stress.

1. SWOT

Put time aside to do a SWOT analysis on yourself in a professional capacity using the form on page 190 of the Appendix. Reflect on and list your strengths, weaknesses, opportunities and threats. Be honest and critical, but not too hard on yourself. Don't forget the positives. If laid out clearly, this will give you a starting point from which to construct an action plan and to see possible goals emerging. Revisit your SWOT regularly and add to it: make it a dynamic document that works for you. If you are comfortable doing so, ask others for their opinions, too.

2. Goals

Identify three main areas that you wish to work on and set SMART goals and an action plan to break your goals down into manageable chunks. Be realistic about what you can achieve and how. Ensure the areas of focus are relevant to you and to the school. Ensure also that you will enjoy learning from them. Remember: a goal may be to learn a new skill or improve upon something, or to make more time for something; it does not necessarily need to involve working on a 'weakness'. If you feel comfortable doing so, it is advisable to share your goals with your peers and your team. There is more chance you will follow them through if others know about them. Some examples of areas to work on may be time management, developing new courses, staff training, stress management, crisis or change management, and project planning.

3. Reflective practice

Just as it is for teachers, this is a powerful tool in looking back and then moving forward in your development. Reflect daily on how you deal with aspects of your job, and consider what you could do differently. This reflection can be linked specifically to your goals but can also be done daily to reflect on how you conduct yourself at work. With this in mind, give yourself praise for what you achieve each day. The life of an academic manager is multi-faceted and sometimes lonely; it often seems as if there is not enough time in a day to do everything. You may feel you have not actually achieved anything on some days. This is rarely true. By reflecting daily on what you have done and what you have achieved, you will leave work feeling positive and ready to start the following day afresh.

4. A critical friend

Having someone at your level to share your developmental journey with is extremely beneficial. A critical friend is someone who asks questions and offers critiques of your work in order to help you succeed in a professional pursuit. Your critical friend should be somebody you trust. It could be an ex-boss or colleague, a former teacher trainer or a peer in another organisation. They do not have to work within your industry, so you can reach out to a broader network.

5. Management training

There are many sources of ELT management training. You can find numerous organisations and forums online, along with various online management communities. British Council English Agenda (https://englishagenda.britishcouncil.org) is one such source of online PD for teachers and managers. It includes useful documents, guidelines and webinars on management, teaching and PD. Find what works for you and dip in regularly, offering support as well as asking for it. There are also formal qualifications, such as ELT diplomas, MBAs and MAs in ELT management. Ensure that you have the time and support from your organisation before embarking on such a project. Alternatively, set yourself a smaller action research project to start with.

6. Outside the industry

Very often, the best guidance and training can come from other sources outside ELT. Join your local chamber of commerce or find out what is available to you locally in the form of management training. We can learn a lot from our peers in other professions and we may even find that in ELT we do certain things well, in comparison. Look at other industries' training programmes in such areas as the training and development of staff, teamwork and customer care. There is a lot of good material available online and face to face, such as the Harvard Business School newsletter. However, do not overwhelm yourself with too much. Take a structured approach to what you decide to do to enhance your PD and make it relevant to your work context.

7. Learn a new skill

You may find yourself doing the same routine week after week once you have mastered your role. Reflect on where there may be room to bring in a new skill. This could come in the form of a new way of doing something, such as communicating with your team, or it could be something completely different, such as taking on some financial or marketing aspect that complements what you currently do. By putting yourself forward like this, you are forcing yourself to learn a new skill on the job. Moving yourself out of your comfort zone will keep you alert and motivated. You are also showing that you are able to grow within your role, thus opening yourself to further responsibility and possibly promotion.

8. **Review and share**

   Factor in meetings with yourself, your critical friend or your line manager to review the progress you have made in terms of the goals you have set, and to decide whether they are still relevant and interesting, or if you should move in a different direction. Analyse how they fit in with your initial SWOT analysis and get feedback from those around you. This will help you to measure whether your pursuits are reaping the benefits you intended for yourself, your team and your organisation. Don't be afraid to scrap a project and start again. Finally, share your accomplishments. Don't be shy. Middle and senior managers often focus on others and forget about themselves: let others know what you, too, are achieving and working towards. Not only is this good for you but also for the profile of your organisation.

9. **Managing your time**

   Your own PD should not create added stress for you at work or at home, so ensure that you manage your time efficiently to incorporate your development in a 'small and often' way. Do not postpone small developmental tasks to the point that they become huge stressful chores. If this is happening, you may wish to review your PD goals, embark on a time-management project or course, or, together with your manager, review your current role, discussing the importance of making time available for your PD. Remember to have some 'you time', too. See Unit 44 on managing yourself.

10. **Act now!**

    You may have read this unit and liked some of the ideas but will delay putting any of them in place. Now is your chance: take five to ten minutes to write down as many areas as possible that are of interest to you in your current and evolving role. Put this list on your desk and, over the new few days, let it develop into a plan. Schedule ten minutes in your diary to do the SWOT analysis referred to in Tip 1, and then ten minutes at some point in the following week to set one to three SMART goals for yourself as a result of your analysis. Now you have taken the first steps on your PD journey in less than half an hour – well done!

> *"Taking time out from the day-to-day running of the team and the wider business for professional development is absolutely essential not only to my own success as a leader and manager but to that of my team. I've never had the time to do an MBA but accessing bite-sized professional development from experts in and out of the industry I work in equips me with the knowledge, skills and confidence to deliver the best I can for my team and business."*
>
> **Leanne Linacre, Director, LILA Liverpool**

10 tips for managing yourself

An ELT management position is rewarding, challenging and often fun, but for new managers it can be a steep learning curve. It is multi-faceted and, at times, all-consuming. For this reason, it is important that you look after yourself. You can only give your best to your organisation and the people you manage if you feel healthy, mentally stimulated and supported, and if you have a good work–life balance. Here are some tips to help ensure that you are looking after your own well-being.

1. Set daily goals

Alongside your bigger-picture goals spread over the year, set yourself small daily goals. Don't overcomplicate this; goals can be as small as managing to speak with a teacher about their performance by lunchtime, with the aim of getting a positive outcome. Be flexible and realistic: will you achieve all your goals in one day? Decide which ones can be saved for a later day if necessary and which ones are crucial. Always leave some 'wiggle room' for the unexpected. Learning what is a priority and what can be postponed comes with practice and experience. If you are not sure, ask a colleague to check your list of what you think you can achieve in one day.

2. Move around

Make sure you are not completely desk-bound all day. As a manager it is easy to get tied up in admin, projects and dealing with emails. Make a point of getting up and going to see your colleagues rather than sending an internal email. If necessary, back things up with an email, but talking face to face builds better relationships and keeps you active. Think of classroom practice: a good teacher would not encourage students to sit down working on one or two tasks all lesson; they would include interaction as well.

3. Identify when you are stressed or overwhelmed

What does your stress look like? How do you know when you are overwhelmed? Learn to recognise signs of these in yourself in order to better manage them. It is never advisable to keep these feelings bottled up. Sometimes you may feel a sense of panic that there is too much to do; if this is the case, share your concerns with someone. You could, for example, talk to your line manager or a colleague. It may be that your line manager or boss is not aware of how much work you have. At the very least they should be able to help you prioritise. Even hearing yourself talking this through can lessen the stress and your perception of the situation. A fresh pair of eyes can often see things differently. Your confidant might be able to advise on how to cope with your tasks and your feelings.

4. Don't stay too long

As a manager, there will be times when you need to put in extra hours, such as in preparation for a school inspection. However, it will be beneficial to your well-being to have enough discipline to know when to walk away for the day. Very often, the later you stay the less productive you are. Switching off and getting rest will be much more beneficial to you and the task you are working on. Ask yourself how productive you are being in those last hours of the day. With this in mind, be aware of what times of day you work best; for example, some people like to tackle jobs that need a lot of headspace (such as course design) at the beginning of the day, leaving the more mundane administrative tasks until later. A nice way to end your day is to have a small regular task such as tidying the teachers' room or writing your to-do list for the following day.

5. Stay fit and healthy

Ensure that you factor in some form of exercise, even if that is simply walking to school and back each day. Exercising often generates good ideas and creativity along with positivity. If you don't have time in your busy day, then think creatively: can some form of exercise or activity be offered to staff in the workplace? Hand in hand with this is ensuring that you are eating well and not grazing at your desk while working on a challenging task. Make time to eat away from your desk at mealtimes. You need to be able to switch off. Apart from anything else, working through lunch and generally overdoing things does not set a good example to your team.

6. Don't take it personally

When managing people, you might encounter hostility, complaints and general dissatisfaction from time to time. Remember that this is not normally directed at you personally. Apart from lessening the burden, this realisation will help you to be more objective when listening to your staff, and therefore help you to put yourself in their shoes and consider how you can help. Try to accept that you cannot solve every problem. Sometimes people just want to let off steam. Give them that space without absorbing their stress.

7. Assessing your role

A management position should be stimulating. Monitor whether it is becoming too admin-heavy, perhaps with too few big projects to stimulate you mentally. It is easy to slip into complacency and to just go through the motions but this is not good for your well-being. Identify what interests you and take on a new challenge – one that will be motivating for you and beneficial to your organisation. This could involve setting up an action research project, becoming involved in an industry working group or developing a new product or market. In bite-sized chunks you should be able to manage this new challenge without letting your day-to-day job suffer. A useful way of assessing your role is to revisit your job description, possibly with a peer or line manager. This should happen as a matter of course with your line manager at your annual appraisal, but you don't need to wait until then to review the situation.

8. **Enjoy yourself**

   Have fun at work. Appreciate your colleagues and take an active interest in them. In the end, they are often the people that we spend most of our adult lives with. The ELT industry is a very social one. Get out of the office, meet your peers who work in other schools, join local ELT groups, accept invitations to events and build a network of supportive friends and colleagues.

9. **Say 'yes' to things**

   Saying yes and being open to new opportunities and challenges will keep you interested in and positive about your job. However, there is a fine balance: you do not want to take on so much that you become overwhelmed. A good question to ask yourself is: 'What is the worst thing that can happen?' For example, you might ask yourself: What is the worst thing that can happen if I say yes to this new project? Then reflect on how you might deal with any negative outcomes. If one outcome might be that you would not be able to finish all your tasks on time, ask yourself whether there is someone else who might be able to take up the slack.

10. **Self-reflect**

    Take time to reflect on your achievements, big and small. It can be a useful exercise to do this in a focused way two to four times a year. It creates a sense of pride in your accomplishments, allowing you to forward-plan knowing what you are capable of. Management can be a lonely place with little glory, so it is up to you to motivate and congratulate yourself. It is good practice each day as you leave work to reflect on all the good things that you have done. There are always plenty once you start thinking about it. It means you finish the day feeling positive and ready for the next one. Don't beat yourself up about things that could have gone better; instead, reflect on what you can learn from them.

> *"Making the wellbeing of ALL staff a priority is the key to a successful institution. It leads to happier staff, better teaching and higher levels of learner attainment. Everyone benefits when an organisation and its leadership put wellbeing at the heart of their guiding principles. It is not an optional extra. It is the foundation of good practice."*
>
> **Sarah Mercer, University of Graz, Austria**

10 ways of networking and developing your own career

Building professional networks is important to the success of your career and can raise your own profile along with that of your organisation. It can open career doors and opportunities as well as providing professional support. Networking is something we can sometimes see as an add-on to our busy role rather than a part of it. However, it is advisable to embrace networking opportunities as a way to benefit and develop your career and learn about business opportunities for your school. Being involved in many aspects of ELT provides a broader knowledge of the overall profession. Being an academic manager shouldn't stop you from attending marketing or business development events and being involved in those circles too. Here are 10 tips on how to network successfully and develop your career.

1. Getting out and about

Join local groups. Some may be industry-specific, but there will be others, such as the Chamber of Commerce and local business networks, that can also provide useful contacts. Joining, of course, is only the first step. It is important to then make time to attend events and talk to people. Set yourself a goal to attend, say, one event every two months and within that a sub-goal to speak to five people during an event.

2. Talking to people

Overcome shyness. This is easier said than done sometimes, but remember that this is a professional situation, and you often find yourself doing things that are not easy in various other aspects of your role. One way of easing social awkwardness is to think of a few open-ended questions to ask when you first meet someone; for example: 'Tell me more about your company/your role/a project that you are working on' or 'How did you get into this industry/line of work?' Show interest, ask questions, give information about yourself and look for common links to keep the conversation going. Politely excuse yourself and move on when you feel the conversation is coming to a natural end. People are not generally offended because, at the end of the day, everyone is there to make contacts.

3. The basics of networking

When meeting people for the first time, ensure you have your business cards. When receiving a business card, don't just put it in your pocket; use it to lead into conversation about the other person's job or organisation. Keep the conversation professional, remembering that you are an ambassador for your organisation, but do also try to show an interest in the person themselves rather than just talking shop. People will remember you more if there is a mutual interest, such as a love for a certain type of sport or a country you have both worked in.

4. Getting known

Put yourself forward for things. Becoming known in the industry is good for your reputation and can also be satisfying. There may be opportunities to become involved in multi-school projects or to sit on committees. Time allowing, such opportunities are rewarding: they enhance your reputation and may lead to further career opportunities. You are also flying the flag for your school and raising its profile. At the same time, you are giving something back to ELT by building the reputation and professionalism of the industry through projects, committees and cross-school groups.

5. Sharing ideas and working together

Be active in local teaching organisations and willing to share best practice (within reason). Get to know other local schools. It can even be beneficial to organise joint events or arrange to take on joint projects. Invite your peers in other organisations to visit you and ask to visit them. This can be a time to show off and be proud of who you are as a school. Your friendly competitors will not replicate your school and your selling points in a visit so do not be overprotective. Just remember you and your school have an identity because of you and your colleagues. Somebody else will do things their way so just embrace making contact, visiting, collaborating and sharing ideas.

6. Moving out of your area of expertise

Put yourself forward to be involved in events or organisations that are not strictly your department. For example, if you are an academic manager, you could occasionally offer to attend student fairs to understand how that aspect of your school works. Clients like to speak to the non-sales and non-marketing people about the product; moreover, it gets you known in a different environment. This in turn gives you more insight into different aspects of your school and the industry. Moving out of one's area of expertise works both ways; marketing managers and other administrative staff will benefit from the opportunity to observe classes and talk to teachers.

7. Moving out of your comfort zone

When attending a conference, put yourself forward to present a talk or workshop. This may put you out of your comfort zone, but ask yourself what's the worst thing that can happen? What you will probably find is that you get a real buzz and a sense of achievement. It is also the best way of becoming known by others and provides conversation points when you meet attendees following your talk.

8. Following up

When meeting people, never miss an opportunity to identify areas of common ground that might lead to some type of future collaboration. With this in mind, we should note the importance of the follow-up. Be sure to send an email following the meeting, summarising any work-related business opportunities that were discussed. This should be done soon after the meeting while the contact is still 'warm'. Keep a note of any personal information about your contacts that may be useful when following up.

9. Building relationships

Think about your interpersonal skills. Normally, you don't have to be too formal during a meeting and in the follow-up (though this may depend on the cultural norms of the person you are dealing with). Importantly, be yourself. If possible, invite contacts to visit your school and learn more about who you are. At the same time, try to be sensitive to your potential contact's priorities: if they seem to be less interested in collaborating than you are, they won't appreciate being pushed.

10. Giving something back

ELT is a very empathetic, people-focused profession. Think about what you can give back to enhance the reputation of the profession and also to help less fortunate students. Doing this will broaden your reach both within your network and as a school. Get involved in charity work if possible. Arrange a few all-staff charity events, provide some scholarship places to students, and get involved in the local community. You will find staff are motivated, and it is a great way of raising your profile and that of your school's – all for a good cause.

> *"My own development as a manager came out of a combination of practice and formal learning. I learned influencing skills as a trade union representative in a school, which later sent me on a two-day appraisal course, when I became a senior teacher. I had the chance to set up a summer centre early in my management career, and this experience, together with formal management courses with the Open University, set me on my path. My policy has always been to make sure that I apply anything I learn formally. I think that giving seminars and writing articles on management topics has improved my own practice in these areas."*
>
> **George Pickering, English UK Diploma in English Language Teaching Academic Director and Senior Inspector, Accreditation UK**

10 non-academic services you may need to provide

The student experience will be all the more satisfactory if every need, not just that of language progress, is fully met. To ensure that this happens, the school must look at providing services which on the face of it have little to do with academic development. However, every aspect of the student experience can be seen as a learning opportunity, whether it be a basic necessity or a welcome luxury. Non-academic services will depend on the local context, but the services listed here are certainly ones that you should consider providing – and aim to derive linguistic benefit from as a by-product.

1. **Cultural assimilation and understanding**

   For students who are studying outside their own country in multilingual groups, it will be especially important to explain, appreciate and work with different cultural norms. Even if students are studying in their own country with fellow students who share the same language, questions of cultural differences will arise from the materials being used and the international outlook that ELT inevitably requires. You can't expect students from other countries to be aware of cultural differences automatically, so diminish the impact of culture shock by explaining in advance what to expect in terms of simple things such as the way to greet people, the times of typical daily events like meals and hours of work and, indeed, all stages of the student journey. Establish and embrace differences. Misunderstanding is often based on ignorance, so discuss any differences openly and non-judgmentally.

2. **Accommodation**

   For overseas students, cultural differences can come to the fore when they are outside the school, particularly when they are in their accommodation, whether it is something that they have found themselves or that the school has provided. Accommodation options need to be explained to students, many of whom may not have lived outside the family home before. Accommodation might be a rented apartment, an offsite or onsite student residence and homestay (where students live as part of the family). For all students, make it clear what to expect from each of these options, such as possible costs for local taxes, a deposit, access to the internet and cable TV, health care and the journey to and from the school. For students living and studying in another country from their own, you will need to explain the different way of life and expectations, including typical food and sensitive areas such as use of the bathroom. If your school is arranging the accommodation, ensure you have an accommodation officer who is not only efficient but also caring and non-judgemental. Living in an English-speaking home or residence can be a valuable way of enhancing language learning. Get this right and the rewards will be worthwhile.

3. **Student counsellor**

   The health and well-being of students cannot be taken for granted. Trained counsellors can provide support on a wide variety of issues such as homesickness, learning issues, loneliness and contraception. They should be available and accessible. All students, even if they are living in their own country, will need to have access to this information. Display it clearly on noticeboards and in handbooks, using visuals and accessible language. Include information on rights to medical and dental care, and don't forget mental health and support groups in general.

4. Special needs

Depending on the country where you work, catering for students' special needs may be a legal requirement. Even if it isn't, considering how you can meet the special needs of people with a physical disability (e.g. a wheelchair user or someone with a visual impairment) or special intellectual or learning needs (e.g. autism spectrum disorder or dyslexia) can be very rewarding – both for your organisation and the individuals concerned. In many ways it is just another aspect of needs analysis. Ensure you see this area as an opportunity rather than a threat. Research the needs of these potential students through the official organisations' websites, and talk to the people themselves and their carers. Look at the barriers in your organisation, both physical and attitudinal, and decide how you can remove them.

5. Travel information

Unless they are studying in their own town or city, students will need to have clear information on travel, not just to and from the school, but also to other destinations within the city including places of interest they might want to visit. They will need to know the various transport routes, how to buy tickets, where to board a bus, how to get a taxi, and whether there are any special deals and discounts for students. For students coming from overseas, you will need to give detailed information on flights or other forms of transport, especially visas and what to expect at borders and immigration. Depending on the scale of your operation, try to have school staff at the airport on days when there are high numbers arriving. Make certain all students have a 24-hour school emergency number to call.

6. Legal advice and support

Sometimes, through no fault of their own, students can find themselves caught up in a difficult situation. Before enrolment and arrival, tell students about the basic laws that they must not infringe (even if they are studying in their own country), for example: the consumption of alcohol, carrying a pocket knife, smoking, driving, crossing the road and respecting other cultures. Give clear information on what to do if they are arrested by the police, and their legal rights in general. If possible, get help from the community in dispensing this sort of information, for example through community police officers. Make sure students always have the 24-hour school emergency number. Reinforce all these points with clear information on noticeboards and in handbooks, using visuals and accessible language.

7. Information on local events and facilities

Students will be keen to know about the neighbourhood where they are studying and the opportunities it offers. They might want to know about the best place to get a coffee, where the nearest supermarket or swimming pool is, a music venue or cinema, or a festival or a football match; the list could be endless. One way you can approach this is to brainstorm facilities and events by going through the alphabet from A to Z (you can involve existing students in this). Presenting local information as an alphabetical list is an effective way of ensuring students discover activities that they may not have considered. Remember that all of these events and facilities can be linked to the learning programme. Accessing the local environment can be an integral part of learning beyond the classroom and can provide many linguistic benefits.

8. Leisure programme

An organised social programme of regular events catering for all interests can be a useful addition to the range of services offered to students. It will build a sense of community and help students develop their language learning and cultural awareness. Aim for a range of events, some in-house (such as a quiz or a film night), some outside the school (such as theatre trips, walks or dinner at a local restaurant). Be sure to consult students. Make someone (often referred to as a 'social organiser') responsible for this part of the programme. It's a role that you can rotate in order to maintain variety.

9. Work opportunities

Many students may want, or even need to, find work. For students not studying in their own country, it is essential to check what they can and cannot do workwise, and to explain local employment laws and employment rights. If students are simply looking for work in order to get extra language practice, suggest that they might consider volunteering (for example in a charity shop or as a teaching assistant). Consider organising your own community projects; for example, cleaning up the local park or planting a vegetable garden in the school grounds.

10. Prepare a brief

Prepare a brief for the production of a new student guide that will provide information on relevant non-academic information, services and facilities. You could focus on your own school or a school that you know well.

Think about the following points. Remember: you are producing a brief, not the actual guide.

- ▶ The areas/topics you want to be included.
- ▶ The format you are going to use, for example electronic, paper, app.
- ▶ The design features you might use: layout, colours, visuals.
- ▶ Ways of making it accessible, for example the level of language used.

You can use the photocopiable form on page 191 of the Appendix to help you record your ideas and thoughts.

10 ways to improve your working environment

Educational managers not only have to manage courses, people and operational procedures, but they also have to manage the working environment where all these elements co-exist. Working environments reveal a lot about the function and the ethos of an organisation. In education, perhaps more than in other sectors, the working environment has to accommodate a range of different functions. All of this provides an opportunity for whole-school activities, which can bring a sense of community and belonging to the students. In some larger operations, such as university departments, the manager may not have the authority or the opportunity to change the working environment in a major way. However, little things can still make a big difference. Asking the right questions is the key to making improvements, and at the end of this unit you will find two activities to help you think about your own working environment.

1. Form and function

We do not always have the luxury of a purpose-built educational building. Sometimes schools are not located in school buildings, and even when they are, the space may have been designed to meet the requirements of a different age or educational sector. Ask some basic questions about what the learners, teachers and other users of the building need from a working environment, and how the physical building where you work influences the way people work, learn and teach. Look at the constraints imposed by the building, and what, if anything, you can do about them. As far as possible, ensure that the physical form of the environment supports and enhances the function and the purpose of the school.

2. Audit your space

Look at the way you use each room, office and physical space in your building. Consider what goes on in each space and what the needs and functions are of the people who use it. Think about whether the room itself enhances those needs and functions or whether it works against them. A quiet room will be needed for confidential meetings and quiet study, but not every space will be quiet, so you will have to make decisions about what you can use noisier rooms for. It is also important to ensure that the location of the offices, classrooms, lounges and other rooms maximise efficiency, communication and comfort. As an experiment, think about the possibility of swapping the use of some of the rooms, for example the teachers' room and student lounge, to see if doing so improves working patterns and conditions.

3. First impressions

You've seen your building a thousand times, but try to see it through the eyes of a first-time visitor. You could, of course, ask a new student about their first impressions, but you could also bring in a first-time visitor and get them to describe their thoughts honestly. During staff induction and training, ask for opinions on the set-up: staff who have worked at other schools may be able to bring fresh insights.

4. Small changes

Small and subtle changes can make a difference: a new display of student work, a board giving learning tips, a photo and bio-data for an individual student or staff member. Even putting a familiar notice in a different place can lead to students becoming more aware of what's around them.

5. Decoration and design rethink

Just because the school has always been the way it is doesn't mean it has to stay that way. Rethink the decoration and display facilities, the colours and design, the way the information is displayed (and whether it is up to date). Ask yourself whether the design and decoration reflect your vision and mission. Involve the students and staff in the project. Make it fun!

6. Big changes

Of course, if the budget allows, you can have more grandiose plans to modernise or expand the building to meet changing expectations. How are you going to be teaching in the future? Still in classrooms? Using shared spaces? You can rethink the internal structures, such as the use of glass walls instead of brick. In an age of galloping digital and mobile technology, you may decide to strip out all the computers in the self-study centre. You can then discuss with everyone in the school what the space could be used for: a games room, a traditional library, a digital hub, a relaxation space.

7. Environmental considerations

Climate change issues and other ecological concerns are often reflected in course materials. It is a simple step to make such course materials specific to the school's own working environment. With the whole school you can build a green agenda, involving the use of less plastic, recycling, encouraging cycling to school and raising awareness in general to help students feel they have some ownership of the environment.

8. Other forms of life

Plants and flowers have a positive effect on the working environment. An aquarium in the reception area is known to be calming and soothing. In primary education for very young children it is quite usual for there to be a class pet, looked after by the children. Shy and nervous students (particularly children) are known to be more relaxed in the presence of small, cuddly animals. Having a school pet, such as a cat or a guinea pig, may not be practical in every school, but it can help make the working environment more relaxed and provide opportunities for incidental language practice.

9. Photo boards

A familiar feature of many language schools is a picture board in a prominent place showing all the staff (smiling, if possible), with a simple description of their role, and why students might need to speak to them. In addition, you could also have a photo board of students (but be careful of privacy rights) or photos of the same staff in more relaxed style (for example, doing their favourite sport or hobby).

10. Linking aspiration to physical form

All language schools have their own ethos or culture, whether they have actively chosen it or whether it has just evolved. Carefully chosen design and artwork can transform your working environment. Aspirations are often expressed in promotional material by abstract nouns, such as co-operation, community, respect, efficiency, intellectualism, professionalism and friendliness. You can reinforce these concepts through physical design, colours and artwork. For example, you might have a welcoming, low-level desk at reception to encourage friendliness, posters of famous philosophers to reinforce 'intellectualism', or glass walls to the classrooms to help create a culture of mutual support and non-intrusive observation among teachers.

Ask yourself how you can improve your working environment. The photocopiable forms on pages 192 and 193 of the Appendix suggest questions to consider when reflecting on this topic. Complete the questions and tasks on your own and with your staff (and possibly even with your students, too).

> "The quality of all your relationships is your only unique asset and something that cannot be outsourced or easily replicated. It is crucial that you cultivate empathy, super strong listening skills and a willingness to say 'yes' to new opportunities."
>
> **Emma Sue Prince, Author and Director of Unimenta**

10 ways to ensure your premises are conducive to learning

There are many ways to support learning over and above actual classroom teaching. One way is to make the premises and the general environment conducive to learning through the physical contents, structure and layout of the space you use. This includes not just the classrooms, but all the spaces in the building and external grounds, including the offices and communal areas. Having signs in English is a good way to start. With careful thought you can produce a learning environment that subliminally develops the linguistic and cognitive skills of the students whenever they are in the school. As with the working environment, which we looked at in the previous unit, a lot can be achieved by simple and subtle adjustments.

1. Classroom basics

The classroom is still the most common learning space. The ideal classroom will be a positive place where a student can focus on learning, facilitated by a teacher. It will be both comfortable and engaging. It will need to be sufficiently spacious to allow different types of interaction, such as pairwork, groupwork and individual study. The room should be appropriately furnished, heated and ventilated with at least some natural light. There should be good sightlines to the teacher, fellow students and any boards or screens (traditional or digital).

2. Classroom layout

In most situations around the world, managers and teachers have little control over the size and structure of the rooms they use. However, you might have influence over the choice of furniture and the best classroom layout for specific learning objectives. Whether you choose rows of desks, a horseshoe configuration, islands of tables, seminar chairs or tables, or a relaxing space with armchairs and bean-bags, you will be facilitating different types of communication. For example, it is common when teaching ESP (English for Specific Purposes) to configure the class for practice activities by simulating the working environment of the specialism, e.g. a café-style layout for waiters or rows of seats with an aisle for flight attendants. The way you arrange the classroom should always be a conscious decision, so discuss these different arrangements with teachers and students.

3. Classroom rules

Any room or space with a specific function will have rules and protocols of behaviour to ensure it fulfils its purpose. For example, think about a supermarket, a hospital reception or a library. In all of these places there are things that you can and can't do. A classroom is no exception. Establish classroom rules and procedures in consultation with the students and the teachers. A good idea early on in the course is to produce a learner contract, in which both students and teachers decide how they are going to work together. Examples of clauses in the contract might be: only speak in English, don't interrupt another student, keep mobile phones face down on the desk. Discussing and deciding on these rules will help with learner training.

4. Own the classroom

It may not be possible for a class of students to have the same classroom all the time – indeed, it may not even be desirable. However, learning will be more effective if the learners have a sense of ownership of the spaces they use. This is sometimes referred to as 'colonising the classroom', with displays of students' work, ideas for effective learning, photographs and objects relating to learning topics (in addition to more conventional displays of course objectives, timetables and other administration notices). It's a good idea to have a rota of students responsible for changing displays.

5. Be visual

Peripheral learning can be a very effective tool, but by its very nature can often be neglected. As a manager, resist the temptation to keep walls clear and empty. Learning can be effectively supported and maintained through the use of visuals and posters. These can come in a variety of forms, for example prompt cards with useful classroom language, often containing gaps: What does ___ mean? How do you spell ___? Could you repeat that? Other visual arrangements to consider displaying are mind maps, or even random lists of key language from previous lessons, with pictures, if possible. Such prompts can help students self-correct.

6. Catering to a variety of learning preferences

You can accommodate learners' diverse preferences by regularly adapting teacher input and learning resources. Represent your awareness of different learning preferences by displaying material around the classrooms and the school as a whole. In addition, there may be particular devices and resources that certain students and teachers find particularly engaging, for example flip-charts, display screens, poster displays, phonemic symbols and charts. Electronic devices are another important tool in the classroom and school. These are discussed in Tips 7 and 8 below.

7. A space for independent learning

If your students are to maximise their learning opportunities, they will need to make use of facilities outside the classroom. Traditionally, this need was met by libraries, computer rooms and learning zones, and many schools still have these spaces. They can easily exist alongside VLEs (virtual learning environments) and other digital learning devices, but as a manager you will need to decide if and how you use them. More and more learners are using their own devices to access the school's VLE, whether by laptop, tablet or smartphone, and you will need to accommodate this practice positively. BYOD (bring your own device) is becoming more common and clearly provides a direct route to independent learning; however, there may be compatibility and connection issues. Virtual or physical, you will still need to make students aware of the importance of independent learning (or self-study) by actively introducing them to the materials and showing them how to use them effectively. This could be done by a simple introductory video, a step-by-step poster guide, an allotted part of the timetable, and a physical place for study and relaxation.

8. A place for technology

Technology in the form of interactive whiteboards (IWBs), data projectors, display screens, laptops, computers and so on will all require space. Think carefully about where you locate these items so that they provide the maximum advantage for students without restricting other forms of input and interaction. Any educational technology inside the classroom or elsewhere should be well maintained and come with adequate technical support. Make sure staff receive appropriate training, and that there are people they can approach if they have problems. Remind students about the learning potential of technology and digital applications outside the school, as well as use of in-house VLEs and applications.

9. Beyond the classroom: the Total Learning Environment (TLE)

The classroom and the VLE are both examples of learning environments. But every environment you find yourself in is potentially a learning environment, and every experience is a learning experience. We are missing an enormous opportunity if we do not exploit the learning environment in the big wide world beyond our classrooms and our school buildings (often referred to as the Total Learning Environment or TLE). Most teachers and language teaching organisations are aware of this potential, but how effective are they at bridging the gap between what happens in the classroom and the vast pool of learning resources beyond? One way to do this is to imagine all of these experiences and environments as items in a resources cupboard. We wouldn't just leave the door open and let them help themselves; we would select and adapt them and guide our learners in how to use them according to their needs and their desired learning outcomes.

10. Look into the future

Managers always need to plan for the future. When it comes to the physical structure of the learning environment, these plans need to be made well in advance. Think back to what classrooms and learning facilities looked like ten years ago. What has changed? Now think about what classrooms and learning facilities might look like in ten years' time. Consider each of the core features of today's learning environment and how they would be different: the position and role of the teacher, the furniture and the layout, what's on the walls, technology and learning resources in general, the types of activities and communication channels, the number of students, learning opportunities outside the classroom, and so on. Does the classroom even exist? You can use table on page 194 of the Appendix to make some notes.

10 key points in safeguarding and well-being

The safety and well-being of your students and staff is something that you need to keep in mind constantly, even though you may be preoccupied with academic delivery and progress. It is easy to overlook this aspect of management, but if you neglect it, you will not only be doing everyone a disservice, you will also be undermining their ability to progress in their learning and teaching.

1. **Duty of care**

   Everyone has the right to a safe and healthy environment and all staff, whether they are managers or not, have a duty of care to preserve this. Ensure that this is made clear in job descriptions and in induction briefings, as well as on noticeboards. Establish effective routines, policies and procedures to achieve this.

2. **Helping and supporting students**

   As a minimum, everyone in your organisation should feel that they have someone to turn to. It doesn't have to be a trained support counsellor. Make certain that students (and staff) know that they can talk to someone and clearly identify the person or people who have special responsibility for this. Include the topic of welfare in questionnaires, in tutorials and in special drop-in clinics by asking direct questions about whether the student is happy, and whether they have any worries or concerns about their work or other aspects of their life. Learn to identify the signs that not everything is right with an individual – and more importantly, learn not to ignore your concerns and walk away. Be sensitive: the person may just be having a bad day, not a major breakdown, so enquire gently to find out.

3. **Safeguarding**

   Safeguarding is an umbrella term and affects everyone – not just children, but vulnerable adults as well. It means looking after people appropriately and helping them to stay safe. It might include medical needs, pastoral care, supervision and security, attention to smoking, alcohol and substance abuse, and e-safety. Child protection is the need to protect under-18s from direct harmful behaviour and forms of abuse, which can be physical, emotional or sexual, or can involve neglect. The precise legal requirements will depend on the country in which you are based, but don't be afraid to deal with issues even if they are not covered by local laws.

4. **Safeguarding training**

   It is important to establish basic principles for safeguarding, even though legal requirements and protocols will differ depending on the country. Safeguarding training courses are available in most countries, and are often delivered online. Training courses will generally include the topics of understanding vulnerability, identifying signs of abuse, an awareness of duty of care, and knowing how to report and refer issues. Particular care needs to be taken with under-18s studying in adult classes, or where under-18s share the same campus as adults.

5. **Tips for how to behave in welfare situations**

   Being sensitive and understanding is important, but remember to keep neutral and detached as well. Find a suitable space; listen, don't take sides, be objective and, if possible, have someone with you. Keep a record of what is said and don't be afraid to refer to other authorities if you are not sure of the best line of action to take.

6. **Handling abusive behaviour, harassment and bullying**

   Different cultures have different approaches to what is acceptable and unacceptable behaviour, so it is important to be clear about what is not acceptable and what the expectations are in your school. Sometimes people think of abusive behaviour, harassment and bullying (including cyber-bullying) as something they have to accept, especially if they are in a foreign country where lots of things are done differently. Make it clear that this is not the case in your organisation. Words like harassment, abusive behaviour and bullying are classed as high level (B2/C1), and will need explanation for lower-level students. Use posters with pictures that make meaning clear. Encourage and expect respect: defining what is meant by 'respect' can be a useful class activity or whole-school project.

7. **Safer recruitment**

   If you teach children (usually those under 18) and vulnerable students in your school, it is important to follow careful recruitment practices. This will mean looking carefully at references and asking referees if they know of any reason why the candidate should not work with children. Criminal record checks will be needed. This may take some time as potential teachers and staff could have been working in different countries, and you will need a police check from each country. Start the process as early as possible and have contingency plans for staff who start work but are still awaiting their suitability checks.

8. **Helping and supporting staff (and yourself)**

   In your concern for the welfare of your students, don't forget your staff and yourself. Get to know your staff and watch for signs of welfare concerns (such as mood swings and problems at home). Remember, however, that there is a fine balance between intrusion and caring. Do the same for yourself and recognise the signs that may mean you need to slow down and adapt your behaviour. Do not be afraid to seek professional support and advice.

9. **Risks and critical incidents**

   Risk management can be divided into two broad categories: everyday risks such as trip hazards and crossing the road, and major crises that you hope will never occur, but that you need to plan and prepare for nevertheless. You need to assess the risks in every aspect of your operation from uneven flooring to unstable walls. And for those you really can't predict, you need to have critical incident protocols in place. Think about the systems and procedures for dealing with risk and crisis that you have in place at your school. Are they effective? Are they used? Are they reviewed and revised? In a major incident, how would you communicate with the people you need to contact?

10. Do a risk assessment

The first rule for producing risk assessments is to understand that they are very important – potentially a matter of life and death. The second rule is that they should be actively used, not just left in a dusty folder or buried away on a computer database. The third rule is to enjoy the process and see it as an opportunity. To help you carry out a risk assessment, use the photocopiables on pages 195 and 196 of the Appendix. The first is an example of a standard risk assessment template for school trips, which you can either use as it is or adapt for your school. The second is a list of possible risks and critical incidents for you to consider. Note also that various organisations such as the British Council, EnglishUK and EAQUALS have risk assessment forms as part of their assessment criteria which you can refer to.

10 things you hope to hear when students (and staff) leave

At the end of a course it is easy to get caught up in the leaving process of issuing exam results and certificates, holding end-of-term parties, celebrations and graduation ceremonies, as well as preparations for the next intake. But at the same time, don't forget to collect and listen to leavers' comments. You can learn a lot from what people say when they leave – and that's in addition to the information gathered more formally in exit questionnaires. You should also listen carefully to what staff members say when they leave.

1. **'My English improved a lot and I got the grades I needed'**
   This is probably the comment we are most satisfied to hear. We have fulfilled our purpose and delivered what was required: job done! Sometimes, particularly on short-stay courses, the extent of improvement may not be evident. As an organisation you may need to help your students identify what they have achieved. This requires setting clear and realistic goals at the beginning of and during the course, measuring and applauding progress, identifying new skills and abilities, and getting the student to see these outcomes and successes (as well as being aware of what they still need to do).

2. **'This was one of the best experiences of my life'**
   It's not just about learning English. Studying in a language school, especially if it's in a different country, can be one of the most formative and enjoyable experiences of a person's life. Remember most students are typically aged from 16 to 30, an age of developing maturity when characters are being shaped, opinions formed, career paths forged and lifelong relationships established. Make sure that what you are providing is contributing to that development.

3. **'I had a great time and made lots of friends'**
   As we said above, it's not just about learning English. For some students, the learning of English is almost incidental to the main aim of meeting new friends from different countries, experiencing a new environment and simply having a good time. There is nothing wrong with having that as your main purpose, as long as it doesn't disrupt the learning process in general (for example, by coming in late every day). In fact, it could be argued that students who are outgoing and enjoying an active social life are more likely to develop communicative skills and benefit from communicative teaching.

4. **'I learnt how to make roast potatoes'**
   This was a genuine comment from a 16-year-old Italian boy studying in the UK. He was a good student, around A2/B1 level, who had progressed well. For him, though, the best part of his experience was outside the classroom, living with an English family and experiencing a different culture and learning new skills – in this case, culinary ones. Think about what is behind this comment: involvement with the family, learning how to cook a typically British dish, the language of listening to and checking instructions from an English-speaking host (with no ELT training), writing the recipe out and sending it to his Italian mother, cooking it for his family on his return, and so on. The communicative exchanges and language skills involved in all of this were hugely beneficial to his development in so many ways. Never think that learning can only take place in the classroom.

5. **'I'll recommend this school to my friends/colleagues'**

   Personal recommendations are a wonderfully cost-effective way of getting new business. Offer to send contact details and publicity to relevant people and organisations. Be sure to find out exactly why they would recommend the school, so that you can emphasise these points in your marketing. You might even be able to use the student's comment and photo as a testimonial on your website or brochure (with their permission, of course).

6. **'I was impressed by how well the school was run'**

   A comment like this is perhaps quite rare, as customers tend to expect that things will be run well and will only comment if they think something falls short of their expectations. Excellent service and administration often goes unnoticed. As a result, if you want to find out if the students think that the school is run well, you may need to ask a direct question.

7. **'This experience will look good on my CV (or resume)'**

   Most students study English not because they want a holiday, but because they are developing their careers and accumulating skills that will help them get better jobs. For business English students, this aim is self-evident, but even if students are not thinking overtly of career enhancement, they should be encouraged to record the experience of a language course on their CV (resume).

8. **'I would like to get involved in ELT as a career'**

   Language schools are often very special places with an atmosphere of communication and camaraderie, and an awareness of internationalism that is attractive to young (indeed all) learners. High-level students may have been inspired by their learning experience to become ELT teachers themselves, so give details of teacher training opportunities. Other students may be interested in different roles, as activity leaders, teaching assistants, computer technicians, administrative staff, marketing co-ordinators, finance assistants, welfare officers and paid interns. You may even consider directly employing one of your students after their course; they will certainly be familiar with the organisation.

9. **'Can you send me an enrolment form?'**

   This is something you definitely want to hear. It not only indicates satisfaction with the course, but also offers a business opportunity. Remember, it may not be for the person who requested it, but for a friend, a family member or a work colleague, so get their contact details. You can encourage this by having enrolment forms available to take away, or a more formal 'send-a-friend' discount offer.

10. 'All the staff were so friendly and professional'

It's the staff in a school (the teachers and the rest of the team) who often determine whether a student's leaving comment is positive or not. For this reason, it's also worth considering the comments of staff members when they leave your school. Like students' feedback, their comments are an invaluable source of information and development opportunities, not least because you might want to re-employ them later.

To consider what your staff might say about the school, look back at the ten comments above and think of their equivalents for staff. Some comments (e.g. 5) might be the same. Some will need modifying (for example, 1 might be modified to 'My teaching improved and I can now teach a wider range of levels and courses'). Finally, think of ten things you don't want to hear when students and staff leave, and, using what you have learnt from all the tips in this book, decide what you would do about each negative comment. You can use the photocopiable form on page 197 of the Appendix to carry out these tasks.

Appendix

Unit 5.10: Transferable skills

Think of and discuss seven skills that a good teacher might have and write them in the first column. Then in the second column, write how these skills might be transferable to a managerial role.

Skills of a teacher	Skills of a manager

Unit 8.1: Are you a manager or a leader?

1. Look at the list of 20 attributes. Divide them into two columns: those you associate more with leadership and those you associate more with management.

being entrepreneurial
planning timetables
providing a vision
avoiding and minimising risk
motivating
setting goals for oneself
being creative
accepting responsibility
innovating
taking risks
seeking excitement
coordinating and directing staff
thinking outside the box
seeking followers
organising systems
welcoming responsibility
setting challenging goals for others
delegating
welcoming challenges
organising and directing students

2. Which of the attributes do you think you have? Choose the three that you are best at and the three that you are not so good at.

Appendix

Unit 8.2: A mission statement and a vision statement

1. Here are two more examples from well-known non-ELT companies:

   ### IKEA
   Mission: To offer a wide range of well-designed, functional home furnishing products at prices so low that as many people as possible will be able to afford them.

   Vision: To create a better everyday life for many people.

   ### TED talks
   Mission: To spread ideas.

   Vision: We believe passionately in the power of ideas to change attitudes, lives and, ultimately, the world.

2. Write a mission statement and a vision statement for your current school and for your ideal school.

Unit 8.4: Different levels of management in your school

1. Make a list of the people responsible for management in your school.

2. What are their responsibilities and job titles?

3. Are their job titles accurate? Suggest alternative job titles that reflect the reality of what they do.

Appendix

Unit 8.6: A SWOT analysis

1. Complete the SWOT matrix for your school or for a school that you know well.
2. Think of three action points you would introduce as a result of your analysis.

S What are your strengths?	**W** What are your weaknesses?
O What opportunities do you have?	**T** What threats do you face?

Unit 8.8: A STEP analysis

1. Complete the STEP matrix for the context in which your school operates. An example is given for each factor.
2. Think of three action points you would introduce as a result of your analysis.

S Social factors	**W** Technological factors
Example: *The demographic profile in the area where you operate is changing and there are many more older people (or younger people).*	Example: *After years of poor digital facilities, the area where you operate now has superfast state-of-the art digital capability.*
O Economic factors	**T** Political factors
Example: *The country where your LTO is based is subject to hyper-inflation.*	Example: *A new government in a non-English-speaking country has decided that English should not be used for official channels.*

Unit 11.8: Template for recording action points

Ref	Item	Action	By whom?	By when?	Progress	Closed
01	Need to invest new IT suite. Students and parents have complained.	01.1 Investigate costs with international suppliers	Chris	12/3	[this column to be actively used to record progress – and for use at subsequent meetings, with dates]	[signed off – and date]
		01.2 Review what our competitors have	Chris	End of April		
02	New coursebook needed for young learners	02.1 Contact publishers for samples	Jane	12/3		
		02.2 Focus group with teachers to assess samples	Jane	26/3 tbc		
		02.3 Consider producing our own material?	Jane & Mike	Early April		

Unit 11.10: Successful and unsuccessful meetings

Meeting	Your comments
Was the meeting successful or unsuccessful?	
What was the purpose of the meeting?	
Who was there?	
What was your role?	
Why in your opinion was the meeting (un)successful?	
What did you do in the meeting to influence things? Did it help or hinder?	
Could the meeting have been done over the phone or online?	
If you had been chairing the meeting, what would you have done differently?	

Unit 14.5: A performance improvement plan

Performance Improvement Plan template

Name of employee/teacher ....

Name of line manager ....

Description of performance concern	
Overall aim of the performance improvement plan	
Start date	
Predicted end date	

Example(s) of underpeformance	Expected standard	Success criteria (i.e. how you will know when performance has improved)	Agreed actions	Support required/ requested	Review	Outcome and further action

Unit 15.5: Interview questions for a teaching position

Here is a selection of questions you could ask at an interview. You can adapt them to suit the job in question.

1. **Background questions**

   What attracts you to this position? How does it differ from your previous job?
   Where do you think you may need additional training?
   What skills are you bringing to the job?

2. **Teaching experience**

   What levels have you taught/do you prefer to teach? Have you taught ESP, business English, young learners, large classes etc?
   What materials are you familiar with?
   How do you adapt them to meet the needs of your students?

3. **Practical insights**

   Describe the stages of a recent lesson you were happy with. What made it successful?
   Describe a time when things have not gone well with a lesson. What could you have done differently?

4. **Linguistic knowledge**

   How would you present and practise the past simple to a monolingual class of 30 children?
   What would you say to a student who asked the difference between *will* and *going to*?

5. **Planning and preparation**

   If you are teaching a new course such as an exam course, how would you find out about it?
   How do you find out about the needs of new students or a new group?
   How do you manage your preparation time with a full teaching timetable?

6. **Classroom management**

   Have you ever experienced a personality clash between two students? Between yourself and a student? Have you ever experienced a culture clash? What did you do? Was it successful?
   What would you do if …?

7. **IT**

   Do you have experience working with interactive whiteboards and other smart devices?
   Describe an effective lesson you have taught where you successfully used either a piece of software or hardware. What do you do when the internet goes down?

8. **Professional development**

   What have you done in the last 12 months to develop as a teacher?
   What are your areas of interest and how would you like to develop further?
   Where do you see yourself in two years' time?

Appendix

9. **Welfare and safeguarding**

What signs indicate that a student may not be happy at school or that there may be an underlying welfare issue?

What can a school do to ensure that there is a safe environment for staff and students?

What would you consider to be inappropriate behaviour by a staff member towards a student?

Have you ever had to deal with bullying in your classroom? What did you do?

10. **Attitude**

What do you do to get to know your colleagues in your workplace?

Give an example of a time when you have gone the extra mile for your school.

If you felt there was a negative atmosphere growing in a staffroom, what would you do? How would you feel?

How do you contribute to a positive working environment?

Unit 16.10: Staff satisfaction survey

Complete this satisfaction survey by carrying out short interviews with staff. Complete the two blank boxes with questions relevant to your organisation and add the person's position, if necessary. For any data collection to be taken seriously by staff, it must be analysed and acted upon, with action points fed back to everyone. Where points raised cannot be acted upon, explain to your staff why not.

Position	Is the school meeting your expectations?	If so, how can the school make things even better?	If not, what suggestions do you have to help the school meet your expectations?	Are you (motivated/ happy/ fulfilled) in your work?			
Teacher							
Marketing Manager							
Administration Officer							

Appendix

Unit 17.1: Suggested contents for staff handbook

Staff code of conduct
Equal opportunities
Health and safety policy procedure
Safeguarding young people and vulnerable adults
Child protection policy
Drugs and alcohol
Data protection
Relationships with students and employees
Blogging and social networking sites
Bullying and harassment
Disciplinary
Capability
Grievance
Payment of salaries and other expenses
Sickness
Holidays
Maternity
Paternity
Compassionate leave
Pensions
Security and confidentiality
Anti-corruption policy
Fire policy and emergency evacuation plan
First-aid policy
E-safety policy

Unit 29.10: Analysing the customer journey

1. Complete the table according to the early stages of your own customers' typical journey.
2. Continue with the customer journey by identifying further stages. At each stage, identify the customer's key concern and the question they will be asking themselves.

Stage	Customer question or comment (amend as required)	What does our school do to answer this question or comment?	Is it effective? Give examples.
1	'I want to learn English.'		
2			
3			
4			
5			
6			
7			
8			
9			
10			
11			
12			
13			
14			
15			

Unit 30.10: Feedback forms

Here are ten questions to ask yourself when producing feedback forms and systems to meet the needs of your school.

Questions to ask yourself	Action to take
1. Which areas of our service do we want feedback on?	For example: *teaching, learning resources, arrival and orientation, welfare services.*
2. Which of the areas in 1 require initial feedback (i.e. in first week)?	For example: *accommodation, general contentment.*
3. How often should we gather feedback on each of the areas listed in 1?	For example: *week one, monthly, every term, at the end of the course.*
4. What form will the feedback take for each of the feedback stages?	For example: *face-to-face interviews, tick-box paper, electronic survey.*
5. What type of questions are we going to ask in each of the feedback stages?	For example: *yes/no questions, open questions, ranking 0–5.*
6. Who will write the questions?	For example: *senior manager, department manager, team of staff members, students.*
7. Who will see the feedback?	
8. How will we deal with and follow up on feedback (negative and positive)?	
9. Who will be responsible for data collation and reporting?	
10. When will we review the feedback system, and who will be consulted?	

Unit 32.10: Questions about handling complaints

Question	Answer
1. What was the complaint?	
2. Was the complaint in writing or face to face?	
3. Who was involved? Who was/were the complainant(s) and who was/were the handler(s)?	
4. Did you make the complaint or deal with the complaint?	
5. Was the SLAGO model followed?	
6. What was the outcome?	
7. Was the outcome satisfactory? Why/why not?	
8. Could it have been handled better? If yes, how?	
9. Could it have been avoided in the first place? If so, how?	
10. What did you learn from it?	

Unit 33.10: Ten things you want to improve in your school

Quality standard	Score (for your school now)	Improvement plan (what are you going to do?)	Review after 12 weeks (your new score)
Example A All students will be welcomed by a member of staff on their first day.	8/10	Ensure continuing standards. Establish how welcoming staff are, and incorporate these skills into induction and ongoing training. Go for a 10!	10/10 (as evidenced by student feedback)
Example B Students are placed in classes appropriate to their level and needs.	3/10	Identify which levels are misplaced. Spend more time on pre-arrival testing and ensure all placement testing is relevant to course content. Consider more training in placement skills for interviewers.	6/10 Some significant improvement, but we need to do more, particularly with spoken skills.
1			
2			
3			
4			
5			
6			
7			
8			
9			
10			

Unit 34.7: Example course review form

Teacher name: ....

Course name: ....

Date: ....

Thank you for teaching on .... course. Please complete the table below. The questions are there to help provide a focus, but please feel free to include other information.

Focus	Area to be addressed	Suggested actions
Materials Should any of the materials be replaced/refreshed?		
Content Was it necessary to adapt the plan to suit your learners' needs? Did you use any supplementary materials that might be included on the plan?		
Balance Is there anything you would have liked more/less of on the plan?		
Learner feedback Which parts of the course were best/least-well received? Did the students suggest anything else to improve the course?		

Appendix

Unit 36.2: Example questions for student tutorials

1. Have you enjoyed learning this week/month/term? Why/why not?

2. What have you learnt?

3. What has been useful for you?

4. What would you like more of/less of in class?

5. On a scale of 1 to 10, how much progress do you feel you have you made this week?

6. Did you achieve your learning goals? If not, why not? What can I/you do to help?

7. What two goals would you like to set for the next tutorial?

8. How do you plan to achieve your goals?

9. Do you have friends in school? Have you made friends?

10. Is there anything else you want to share with me about your learning, your concerns or your experience in the school?

Unit 36.7: Student progress review form

How much progress do you think you have made since your last review?

Area	1–10 (where 1 is low and 10 is high)	Reflection notes	New goal	Teacher comments
Speaking				
Listening				
Using new vocabulary				

Appendix

Unit 37.8: Learner autonomy for teachers

Instructions for the manager using the form on the next page

Introduce this approach to your teachers and discuss the aims and benefits. This will only work if teachers take ownership of it. You may decide to elaborate on the simple table shown and divide the record into sections.

Discuss with your team whether they wish to share this at review meetings with the academic manager, and also for it to be used at their appraisal, or whether it is a completely private document.

Encourage teachers to work with the document online. Without taking a top-down approach, remind teachers to complete their record and reflect regularly. This could be done for five minutes at each teachers' meeting, and then you could ask if anyone would like to share anything. This will lead to discussion and will also ensure that teachers focus on it. It is all too easy for the teacher to have good intentions of competing their record but without habit-forming, it may not happen.

Record your own CPD

Instructions to the teacher: decide on a regular day when you complete this form and when you will revisit and add to it. Take time to reflect on how much you are achieving. Consider whether your focus is right and if you are seeing a difference. See the examples in the first two rows of what you might write.

Date	Activity	Impact	Further steps	Review date	Further notes and reflection
	Peer observation	I learned not to be so controlled with higher levels.	Experimentation and share lesson plan ideas with my peer partner.	2 weeks' time	
	Attended a British Council webinar on pronunciation	Noted 2 ideas to use in my B2 class	Implement these into my lesson this week and ask students for feedback.	End of week	

Appendix

Unit 38.1: Lesson observation templates

Do you have a template or set of guidelines you use for observations? Do you adapt it depending on the reason for the observation or the focus of the lesson. Like most developmental documents, the lesson observation template should be a fluid working document. Revisit yours and decide if anything has become dated or not relevant. Decide if you still like the layout. Test out your new document and ask observees for input and feedback. See below some suggested areas to include.

Sample observation prompts

Areas to look for	Observer comments	Observee comments
Preparation		
Presentation		
Challenge		
Flexibility		
Pace		
Staging		
Achievement of learning outcomes		
Error correction		
Feedback		
Subject knowledge		
Pronunciation work		
Classroom management		
Use of resources		
Learner training		
Individualisation		
Cultural sensitivity		
Rapport		

Unit 38.6: Evidence-based observation: example feedback chart

Focus on:	Frequency
Eliciting	18
Giving explanations	18
Giving answers	17
Concept questions	10

Unit 38.8: Suggested action research project procedure

- Self-observe with detailed lesson plan – holistic view to look at the lesson as whole.

- Identify one area of teaching to focus on at first from self-observation.

- Self-observe again with a focus on that specific area – what you like to do better.

- Give yourself thinking time to focus on how to improve or develop. Do research: read, talk to colleagues, observe peers, talk to academic managers, read teacher blogs.

- Try out and experiment with new ideas.

- Analyse again. Keep a record.

- Make a deduction.

- Incorporate into everyday teaching.

- Do further, more in-depth research and share it in the form of a teaching seminar in-house and/or at a teachers' conference. Alternatively, write an article.

- From the observations you make and conclusions you reach, set two teaching goals and one professional development goal to be achieved in a given time.

Unit 39.1: Suggested appraisal questions

General questions

1. Do you feel you have met the standards of your job description?
2. Are there any updates to your job description that you feel should be made?
3. Do you understand and agree with the values of the school?
4. What aspects of your work have been good/bad/satisfactory over the last year? Why?
5. What are your main achievements in the past year? How can we/you build on these?
6. What areas have been difficult or challenging this year? Why? How can you improve on these? How can we support you?
7. What areas do you feel you need more development in?
8. What have you learnt in the past year?
9. What training have you participated in? What would you like to do more of?
10. Give examples of how you have added value to the school
11. Did you achieve your goals in the last period? If not, what could have helped you achieve them? What did you learn?
12. Identify three SMART goals you would like to set for the coming period.
13. What support can we put in place to help you achieve your goals?
14. Are you satisfied with your work–life balance? What changes, if any, would you like to make?
15. What makes you happy at work? What frustrates you?
16. Where do you see yourself in three years' time?
17. What do you think of communication systems in the school? How could this be improved upon?
18. What suggestions do you have for improvements to the school? Think of systems, products, structure, etc.

Teacher-specific questions

1. Which courses have you enjoyed most/least over this period?
2. Which new courses are you interested in teaching?
3. What aspects of your job outside the classroom do you enjoy/get frustrated with?
4. Comment on student feedback over this last period. Are you happy with it? How can you build on it?
5. What do you consider to be your strengths as a teacher? How can you build on these?
6. What do you identify as your main areas for development as a teacher?

Appendix

Manager specific questions

1. Has managing your team over this period been good/bad/satisfactory? Give concrete examples.

2. Can you give an example of a time when you showed good management and leadership?

3. Can you give an example of a time when you could have managed better? What did you learn from this?

4. What are the challenges involved in working with your team? How can you work to overcome these? What support do you need?

5. What do you enjoy most about managing your team?

6. What goals, plans and projects do you have for your team this year?

7. What has your team achieved over this period?

8. How do you think your team would describe your management style?

Unit 40.10: Monitoring staff performance

Here are six ways to monitor and measure staff performance.

1. Be present and interested. Take time to speak to staff, observe how they are getting on, join them in the coffee breaks. This gives you a great insight into how both individuals and the whole team are developing and getting on with their role as teacher.

2. Carry out classroom observations. These allow you to monitor and measure performance against concrete goals and criteria.

3. Analyse student feedback. You may choose to quantify this and feed back to staff. There are several factors to take into consideration with feedback; although measurable feedback can provide a good picture of performance, it should be looked at along with other measures of progress.

4. Carry out appraisals and interim appraisal meetings; monitor goals.

5. Notice evidence of people going the extra mile. Of course, you do not want your staff to go above and beyond all the time as that will lead to burnout. However, it is good to notice (and reward) a staff member when they do go that extra mile for a student, colleague or the school.

6. Use key performance indicators (KPIs). A KPI is a definition of how and when an organisation knows that a standard has been reached. This is possibly easier to define in administrative roles, where success can be quantified (for example, you can count the number of bookings a salesperson takes in a month) as opposed to the world of teaching and learning. KPIs should be clearly defined and made known to staff from the recruitment stage. When robust, KPIs are a useful tool in measuring staff performance and recognising under-performance. They should be objective and measurable; for example: *Student placement is done to a satisfactory standard when all students are tested and placed in the most appropriate course for them in a timely fashion, and paperwork is accurate.*

Unit 41.10: Ten ways of encouraging professional development for teachers

Sample list of CPD opportunities:

- ▶ Teacher conferences (local and international, face to face and online)
- ▶ Local CPD groups
- ▶ In-house CPD sessions (attending and running them)
- ▶ DoS observation (working with DoS to identify areas for development)
- ▶ Peer observation
- ▶ Pop-in observations (short observations of colleagues to see a variety of types of lesson)
- ▶ Self-observation
- ▶ Reflection (daily or weekly lesson journal)
- ▶ Online support (blogs, portals, publisher sites, examination board sites)
- ▶ Idea-sharing discussion groups (in school and online)
- ▶ Mentor or buddy system
- ▶ Trial a new idea one day a week
- ▶ Shared board for classroom ideas and activities in teachers' room
- ▶ Reading (journals, blogs, teacher development books)
- ▶ Writing (write an article or blog post)
- ▶ New projects, courses, levels, teaching trends
- ▶ Action research

Unit 42.5: KWL chart

What do you already **know** about the topic?	What do you **want** to know about the topic?	What have you **learnt** about the topic?

Appendix

Unit 43.1: SWOT yourself

Take the time to look at yourself in a work capacity. Be honest. Don't be overly harsh and don't be too modest. Allow yourself to look carefully both at your skills and at the gaps in your knowledge. This will enable you to make a developmental plan of action.

Strengths	Weaknesses
▶ Good at nurturing positivity and encouraging people. ▶ ▶	▶ Can take things personally. ▶
Opportunities	**Threats**
▶ Provide training to potential new markets. ▶ ▶	▶ Burnout if I don't watch my time management. ▶ ▶

Unit 46.10: Prepare a brief

Ten questions to ask yourself when preparing and designing a student guide to non-academic services:

Question	Your plans
1. Who will be involved in preparing the brief?	
2. What areas do we want to include?	
3. Which are the most important?	
4. How do we want to present the information (e.g. by subject, alphabetically, using visuals)?	
5. How will we make this guide available to students (e.g. print, poster display, app, VLE, website)?	
6. Which information do we suggest students download to their own mobile/electronic devices?	
7. What design features will we use (e.g. layout, colours, visuals, branding)?	
8. How will we ensure the level of language is accessible to all students?	
9. How will we test and trial the content and design?	
10. When will we review the guide?	

Unit 47.10 (1): Discussing the working environment

Here are ten questions to ask yourself about your working environment.

Question	Staff ideas	Student ideas
1. What do learners, teachers and other users of the building need from a working environment?		
2. What are the constraints imposed by your working environment?		
3. How do these constraints influence the way you work?		
4. Does the room where you spend most of your time help you achieve what you want to achieve?		
5. Which facilities and people do you need to be near to?		
6. Think of two rooms in your school: what would be the implications of swapping them?		
7. Does the design and decoration of the school in general reflect the vision and mission of the school?		
8. Do you think your working environment will be fit for purpose in ten years' time?		
9. If you could change one thing about the building, what would it be?		
10. So why don't you change it?		

Unit 47.10 (2): Ten values you want to encourage

1. Think about the concepts and principles you want to encourage in your school.
2. Produce a list of ten abstract nouns that reflect your aspirations for the culture and ethos of the school.
3. Think about how you might achieve these aspirations through physical changes to the buildings, the design and decoration, the use of wall space and colour, etc.

Aspiration	What we already do	What more could we do	What's involved
Example: Friendliness	Example: Smiling staff on arrival / Bright colours in reception	Example: Make the front desk more accessible (eye contact) / Coffee machine in the entrance lobby	Example: Re-design the desk (make it lower) / Reinforce customer service training / Cost of coffee if we make it free
1.			
2.			
3.			
4.			
5.			
6.			
7.			
8.			
9.			
10.			

Unit 48.10: Look into the future

Area	What does it look like now?	What will it look like ten years' time?
Basic description of the premises and learning environment		
Classroom size and layout		
Description of what's on the walls and other classroom resources		
Type of communication in classes		
Extent of independent learning, including digital		
Role of the teacher		
Actively used technology		
Out-of-class learning		
Description of non-teaching facilities		
Are we ready for the future?		

Unit 49.10 (1): Risk assessment form

You can use this form or adapt it for your own risk assessment of facilities at your school, a school visit or accommodation, for example.

What could cause an injury? (e.g. use of the school's garden)	Who could be injured? (e.g. students, staff)	How high is the risk of injury? (e,g, low, medium, high)	How can the danger of risk be reduced? (e.g. remove certain objects)

Appendix

Unit 49.10 (2): Risk and crisis scenarios

Either working on your own or in a group, consider and comment on these possible scenarios. Then consider what action is needed to reduce the risk. Finally, consider how many of the scenarios might be relevant to your school and what measures are needed.

Scenario	Comment	Action/additional control measures needed
Your school does not have a crisis management plan or any risk assessments (apart from fire evacuation drills).	Not having a crisis management plan or other contingency plans is a crisis in itself. Putting one in place should be an operational priority, together with specific assessment of all potential risks and control measures. Risk, health and safety should also be regular items of discussion in meetings and within teams.	
A serious fire breaks out in one of the main teaching blocks.	Induction briefings and regular fire drills at different times, together with trained fire marshals and updated fire safety systems should ensure all reasonable precautions are in place.	
Major roadworks in the vicinity of the school prevent staff and students getting to the school/campus in less than three hours.		
A major security incident takes place in a shopping centre next to your school. Gun shots have been heard.		
Not enough qualified teachers have been recruited for the start of academic programme.		
Course materials required for the new academic year are going to arrive six weeks after the start of term.		
There is a major breakdown of all IT systems with no prospect of repair for two weeks.		
A group of international students are seriously injured in a coach accident when on a school trip in the UK.		
There is a serious outbreak of food poisoning in your school with several students and staff members hospitalised.		
Think of your own scenario.		

50.10: What people say about your school

Student comment (positive)	Staff comment equivalent	What you don't want to hear	What you can do about it
My English improved a lot and I got the grades I needed.	My teaching improved and I can now teach a wider range of levels and courses.	I didn't make any progress at all.	
This was one of the best experiences of my life.			
I had a great time and made lots of friends.			
I learnt how to make roast potatoes.			
I'll recommend this school to my friends/colleagues.			
I was impressed by how well the school was run.			
This experience will look good on my CV/resume.			
I would like to get involved in ELT as a career.			
Can you send me an enrolment form?			
All the staff were so friendly and professional.			

Appendix

10 Tips of your own

10 Tips of your own

10 Tips of your own